YOUTH AND LEADERSHIP TRAINING IN THE NIGER DELTA
The Ogoni Example

Sonpie Kpone-Tonwe

Onyoma Research Publications

© 2003 Sonpie Kpone-Tonwe

All Rights Reserved
No part of this book may be reproduced, stored in a retrievable system or transmitted in any form or by any means, electronic, mechanical, photocopying, recording or otherwise without the prior permission of the author

ISBN: 978-36122-2-0

Published in 2003 by
Onyoma Research Publications
11 Orogbum Crescent, GRA Phase II
P.O. Box 8611, Port Harcourt, Nigeria

P O Box 893, Yenagoa
P O Box 126, Nembe
Bayelsa State, Nigeria

E-mail: kala_joe@yahoo.com
Website: www.onyoma.org

Printed by
Isengi Communications Limited
Lagos & Port Harcourt

Word Processing:
Elizabeth Nwankwo
& Priscilla Kagbaranen
Type Selection and Layout:
Jigekuma Ayebatari Ombu
at Hisis (Publishing) Ltd • Port Harcourt

Dedication

To my amiable daughters:
Leyo, Lebeabu and Baridabdoo,
The *Trio* from whom I learned
First-hand the qualities of
The youths of this dream

Preface

This book is one of a series of publications based on a wide-ranging in-depth research I carried out in the Ogoni region of the Niger Delta, between 1981 and 1990 with grants from the University of Port Harcourt. The book looks at the organization of Ogoni society from pre-colonial times to the present, from the perspective of youth leadership and training. It shows that the *yaa* tradition determined social class structures in Ogoni polity. Youths who had gone through the *yaagẽ* traditional training could advance steadily on the social ladder, while those who had not, remained at the bottom. By its teachings and discipline, the *yaagẽ* tradition discouraged anti-social behaviour among the youth, and inculcated in them a sense of personal holiness and an attitude of generosity, friendship, hard work, diligence, creativity, and good character.

The book reveals that by offering a series of social titles for youths of ability, the *yaagẽ* tradition created the norms of leadership, political hierarchy, and a basis of social mobility. Positions such as house head, village head, membership of elite clubs, etc., became the prerogatives of men who had undergone the *yaagẽ* traditional training. By inculcating in the youths the principles of self-discipline, proper use of tools and weapons, and a knowledge of the arts and the manly occupations, the *yaagẽ* tradition served as a means of constant recruitment for the survival of society and a guarantee for continuity and progress.

The book draws a contrast between the youths of the *yaagẽ* tradition and the youths of the modern organizations in the Niger Delta and Nigeria, and shows that the modern youth organizations lack firm historical and cultural roots. They are therefore deficient in the norms and rudiments of a progressive society. Accordingly, they exist as mere appendages of the contemporary political establishments, which exploit them for purposes detrimental to the society, to the nation, and to the youths themselves. The book argues that unless something is done quickly to reverse the situation, Nigeria's future will remain in jeopardy.

The book concludes by showing that the principle and discipline of the *yaagẽ* tradition constituted an excellent material for turning around the fortunes of our youths for the betterment of the country, and recommends its documentation and adoption into the nation's educational system.

My thanks go to Marv-Yobs Foundation, which granted me a sabbatical and the facilities which enabled me to write this book. 1 am also indebted to Professor E.J. Alagoa, FHSN, JP, OON, FNAL, KSC, who not only supervised my doctoral dissertation but also gave me direction and found time to read through an earlier version of this work and offered useful suggestions. My thanks also go to Dr. A.M. Okorobia of the Department of History and Diplomatic Studies, University of Port Harcourt, who provided information on youth organizations among the Ijỏ of the Niger Delta; and to Jeremiah Mbadiwe, a graduate student of History and Diplomatic Studies, who supplied information on the lkwere (Ikwerre) of the Niger Delta mainland; as well as to my numerous undergraduate students, who contributed in one way or another to make the writing of this book a reality.

My indebtedness is also due to the many informants, who co-operated with me during my field work and willingly supplied the information available to them from the ancients, which has gone into the making of this book. l list hereunder the names of all those whose contributions have been cited in this book.

Others whose contributions have not been cited, will be acknowledged in subsequent publications: His Majesty J.P. Bagia JP, Gbenemene Gokana (d.); His Majesty Ngei A.0. Ngei, JP, Gbenemene Eleme (d.); His Royal Highness G.N.K. Giniwa, JP, Gbenemene Tuatua Tee; His Royal Highness D.D. Deemua, JP, Gbenemene Bua Boue; His Royal Highness J.D. Osaronu, LLB, PhD, Gbenemene Bua Onne; His Royal Highness Atangsi Deebari Tornwe III, JP, Gbenemene Nobana Uwegwere Nobana Kono; Chief J.P. Tigiri of Bien Gwaara (d.); Chief E.B. Nyone JP, of Lewe, Gokana; Chief 0.0. Ngofa, JP, of Aleto Eleme; Chief Mbaedee Francis Mpeba of Nyogo Luekun (d. 1989); Chief John lwagbo, Priest of Nama (d.); Chiefs G.N. Loolo, JP, and J.B. Yomii both of Ko (d); Prince Frederick Buebaa Teedee of Gure (d.); Prince Isaanee Nii of Eepie, Boue (d. 1985); Chief Oji Awala JP, of Ogale, Eleme; Chief Koobee

Asoo of Uwegwere, Boue (d.); Chief Na'ue Lconard Opusunju of Kono (d.); Chief Leelee Naabee Ngito of Kpuite, Tee (d.); Chief Dominic Anderson Keekee of Kpong (d.); Chief Teetee Edamni Nwilabba of Bôo, Ko (d.); Chief Frank Iwerebe of Uwegwere, Boue (d.); Chief M.N. Akekeue, JP of Kpuite, Tee; Chief Nnaa Kpugita of Keneke, Boue (d.); Chief Ipiagbo Kiriki of Tego Town, Boue (d.); Chief Kpoko Kinanwii of Tego Town, Boue (d.); Chief Adoo Gbarato of Nobana Town, Boue (d.); Chief Agbebe Naasah of Kwaakwaa, Boue; and Chief Lemue Nuaka of Tego Town, Boue (d.).

Finally, I give thanks to the Almighty God, who, by His Holy Spirit, gave me the insight and a penetrating mind to understand things that happened so long ago and made them as real to me as though they happened yesterday!

Sonpie Kpone-Tonwe
Department of History and Diplomatic Studies
University of Port Harcourt
May 2002

Contents

Preface		v
Chapter One	Introduction	1
Chapter Two	The Structure of Ogoni Society	19
Chapter Three	The *Yaagẽ* Tradition	25
Chapter Four	Field Activities	31
Chapter Five	Historical Origins Background and Impact	45
Chapter Six	Impact on Modern Youth Organisations in the Niger Delta	55
Chapter Seven	Conclusion	81
REFERENCES		87
BIBLIOGRAPHY		97
APPENDICES		103
Appendix I		105
Appendix II		125
Appendix III		129

Chapter One
Introduction

1. Traditions of Origin

The Ogoni occupy the mainland fringe bordering the Eastern Niger Delta, between the Imo river on the east and north, with the Opobo and the Ibibio across the Imo river on the east, the Igbo on the north, the city of Port Harcourt and the Ikwerre, on the west, and the Bonny, Okrika, and Obolo (Andoni) on the south.

According to the tradition, the Ogoni ancestors migrated from ancient Ghana. Linguistically, however, they are classified as a distinct group within the Delta-cross sub-branch of the Cross River branch in the New Benue-Congo family of the Niger-Congo phylum.[1] Their occupation is mainly farming but some of them are traders and fishermen. The Ogoni have a rich culture and tradition which have remained largely intact, despite their experiences under British colonial rule.

The tradition states that their ancestors migrated from ancient Ghana during a civil war in parts of that ancient empire under the leadership of their empress named Kwaanwaa.[2] According to the account, the group consisted of specialists, including warriors, spirit-mediums, priests, medicine men, etc. After fighting and wandering in the hinterland for years, they finally arrived on the Atlantic coast, where they made canoes. In the canoes, they travelled along the Atlantic coast until they came to the territory now called Ogoniland and settled at a place called Nama on the coast.

Obviously, they carried some effective tools and weapons, which enabled them to establish a settlement at their immediate point of disembarkation to begin a life of agriculture. Without such weapons and tools, they probably would have lived by wandering and gathering, in which case, they would have scattered far from their point of disembarkation and, perhaps, disappeared among the aborigines with whom they later came into contact, or perished in the harsh wild environment. Thus we can see that they were both farmers and makers of sea worthy canoes from very early beginnings. Based on the linguistic evidence, it appears they have thus been settled in their present location from as early as 15 B.C.[3]

A *cliché* recorded in Ogoni oral tradition shows that their ancestors had carried from their place of origin a story of the 'silent trade', first described by Herodotus in the fifty century B.C.[4] The name 'silent trade' was given to the trade by Western scholars, because the parties involved in the trade did not have personal contacts or see each other face to face. Herodotus noted that the trade took place in the upper Guinea coast between the Carthaginians and the Africans of that region of the Old Ghana empire. According to him, the Carthaginians came by sea through what he called the "Pillars of Hercules" or the modern strait of Gibraltar. When they arrived on the coast of Upper Guinea, they raised a huge column of smoke on the beach to announce their arrival. They then placed their wares (mostly red cloth) on the beach, each person's own in its place and withdrew to their vessels. The Africans, among whom were the Ogoni ancestors came out with gold dust, each person placing his own gold against the wares or merchandise of his choice and withdrew.

The Carthaginians came up from their ships and inspected the gold. If they thought the amount of gold was worth their goods, they took it and went their way, if not, they withdrew again without touching the gold. The Africans came down again and added more gold. This was repeated until the parties on both sides were satisfied.

According to Herodotus, there was no cheating by any party on either side. At the end of the transactions, the trading or market for that occasion came to a close.

In Ogoni oral tradition, the trade is called *Du Bari le nēe* ("trade of God and men"), so-called because the Africans thought that the Carthaginians were the "children of the sun god" (piá wĩi Zue) because of the colour of their skin, which was red like the colour of a tropical evening sun.[5]

In the fifteenth century A.D., a Portuguese named Duarte Pacheco Pereira described a weapon carried by a people he had seen in the Eastern Niger Delta (present Rivers State). Pereira noted that the people were "warlike" and that he had not seen their type of weapon elsewhere except "like those of the White Moors of Berbery".[6] Then in 1699, James Barbot visited the same region and made an engraving of the weapon.[7] This writer has elsewhere identified both the weapon and the people as Ogoni.[8] The implication is that the Ogoni ancestors acquired the weapon during their participation in the silent trade with the Carthaginians, the ancestors of the Berbers, before they migrated from the old Ghana empire to their present location in the Eastern Niger Delta. The evidence corroborates both with the date of Herodotus' description and the linguistic evidence.

Furthermore, Walter Rodney has also brought out another vital evidence which was recorded by a Portuguese traveller, Dornelas, who collected it from the elders of Sierra Leone, as tradition handed to them from their grand parents. They told the story of invasions some centuries back, of a people from the Old Ghana empire, whom they called the "Manes", whose army was commanded by a woman. The account states:

> The original chief of the Manes was a woman. She was a leading lady in Mandimansa, Macarico by name, who offended the emperor and had to leave the city. She took with her large numbers of friends, relatives, and dependants, who were transformed into a conquering army. This army overran vast territories and many nations, and its ranks were swelled with recruits...
> When she reached the Atlantic, she divided the army into three parts: one part marched along the coast, the second part marched parallel to it some forty miles inland, the third part marched equidistant on the right flank. (Quoted by Rodney, 1967:224)[9]

Notice how closely the above description corroborates with Ogoni oral tradition, which raises some pertinent questions. Were the Ogoni ancestors part of the Mane army? Who were the Manes? Was the Empress Macarico, Commander of the Mane army, the same woman as Lady Kwaanwaa, Commander of the exploring Ogoni ancestors? When did these events take place?

If all the foregoing evidence point to one thing, it is the fact of the early settlement of Ogoni in their present location. How then was it possible for such a relatively small group of people to survive in such a hostile environment? The answer is to be found in the Yaa tradition, which had kept the Ogoni youths a virile and disciplined lot right from the time of the ancestors. Throughout the rest of this book, our efforts will be concentrated on the Yaa tradition as an institution of youth discipline and leadership training in Ogoniland, with a comparative analysis of similar institutions in the rest of the Eastern Niger Delta and, possibly, in the wider Nigeria.

There are three titles in the *Yaa* tradition. the first and second titles, namely *Piá Gbara* and *Kabaari* are dealt with in this book. The third and highest or the ultimate title in Ogoni known as Gbèné has been treated in an article titled: *"Politics of the Gbene Title in Pre-colonial Ogoni"*.[10] These three titles constitute the core or soul of the Ogoni Personality. They embody the history and a philosophy which goes back to the very beginning of their existence. By the first decades of the twentieth century, the Yaa tradition had begun to decline. In the 1950s, when this writer took part in the tradition as a boy, it was being performed frequently. The interval between two performances was not more than three to four years, depending on the level of prosperity among the leading men of the society. Today, the Yaa tradition is virtually non-existent. Only a few persons who had performed the tradition are alive today.

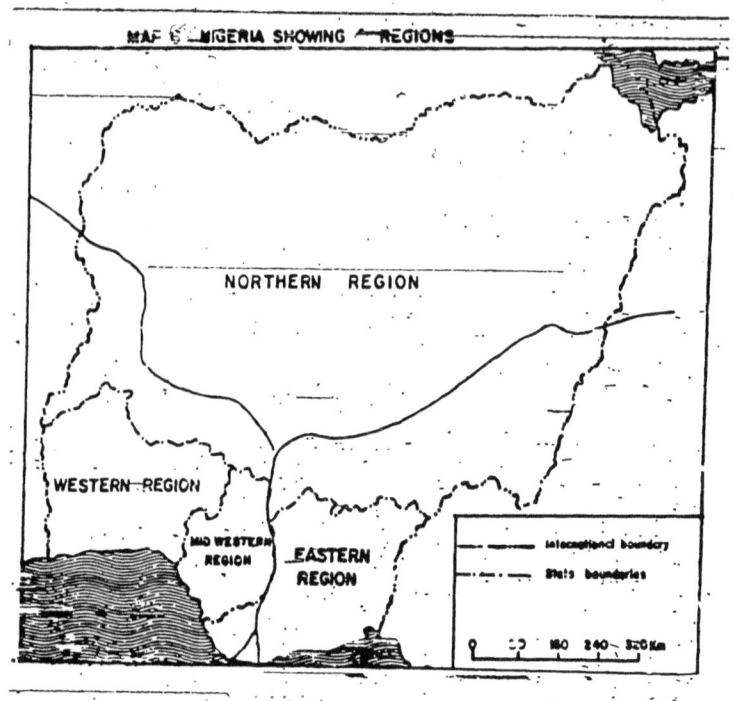

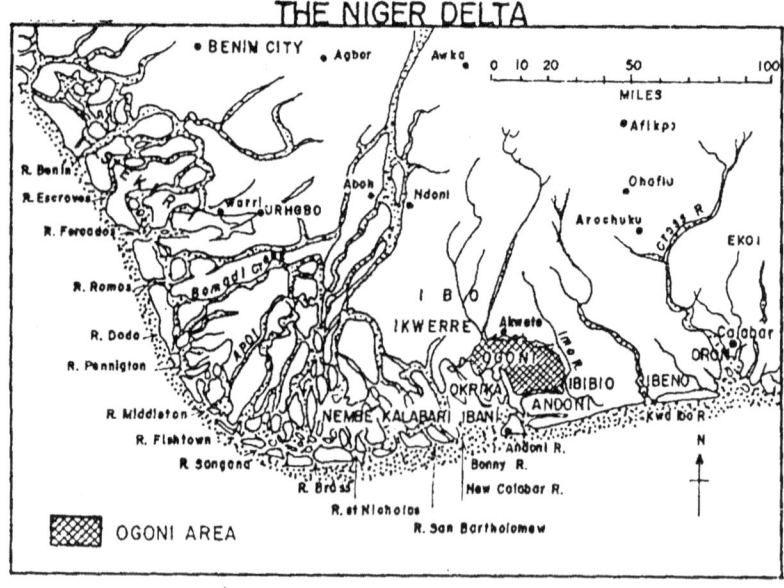

From the 1950s, the next time it was performed was about the 1960s. And of the last two performances, one was in the late 1970s and the other in 1983. I was fortunate to have interviewed the last two performers. Chief Dike Iyoro of Boue, who performed the *Yaawīi* in 1983, was interviewed in February 1984, and Chief Gbenegbara Gookinanwaa, of Uweke, Tee, who got the Gbene title in the 1970s was interviewed in March, 1984. Both have since passed into the realm of spirits. It is ominous that since 1983, no other performance of significance has taken place. In 2000, Chief Tax Kue of Boue did a token performance but it was only a token performance, as the number of youths enrolment was insignificant and the charisma of the performer was wanting. There is no likelihood that another performance will take place in the foreseeable future.

Many factors have contributed to the fateful decline of this great tradition of the Ogoni people. The first began early in the last century with the coming of the Christian missions. The Christian teachings which forbade a number of traditional practices, had very negative impact on the principles and practice of the Yaa tradition. However, judging by the relatively small percentage of conversion to Christianity at that time, the negative impact of the Christian teachings should have been minimal. But there were other negative factors. Ogoni is very near to Port Harcourt, a port city and an oil centre; and from the 1970s, Onne, a south-western Ogoni town, has also been made an ocean terminal and an industrial base. South of Ogoni also, is Bonny Island which, apart from being an ocean terminal, has also become the home of the huge multinational Nigeria

Liquefied Natural Gas (NLNG) Company. The population of these places have not only increased tremendously but have also become cosmopolitan. Consequently their modern influences have adversely affected the *Yaa* tradition.

The greatest of these modern influences was western education. Western education changed the norms of social stratification in Ogoniland. A certificate in Western education became the means of social recognition and a passport to better life. The school teacher replaced the house father of the Yaa tradition and the village school replaced the palm wine camp. And more recently, the radio, the TV and the video cassettes have replaced the lectures, teachings and demonstrations by the elders. Gradually, the youths have been estranged from the local traditions and drawn away to the wider world of the cities. More and more parents have been persuaded to send their sons and daughters to school rather than spend their resources on the *Yaa* tradition.

Still other factors which have contributed to the decline of the *Yaa* tradition, were changes in life-style, in social values, and in the economy. Since the beginning of the last century, life-style in Ogoni has changed significantly. People now place priority on luxury goods such as chieftaincy gowns, hats, shoes, walking sticks etc., rather than on permanent wealth. The change in life-style and social values has also affected the fabric of the economy. People now prefer wage labour (i.e. if they can find it) to owning and working on a farm. The result is that the level of agricultural production has fallen. And the environmental effects of oil exploitation by the multinational corporations, such as Shell, Mobil, Chevron, Agip etc., have aggravated the situation.

Perhaps the most insidious of all these negative impact has been the advent of military rule. During the last thirty years, many traditional values and systems have been adversely affected. People from all sorts of background have been uplifted in society without regard to legitimacy or achievement but based on mere connections. Thus people from all sorts of background have taken the title of Chief without the prescribed traditional qualifications. This has bastardized the traditional titles and values. Because of this, people are no longer prepared to go through the rigours and hardship which tradition required before one could *earn* the title *Kabaari* (Chief). Thus when all these factors are summed together, we find that the forces of change against the *Yaa* traditions are overwhelming and can hardly be reversed. It is against this backdrop that I decided to collect the information about the *Yaa* tradition in an attempt to rescue its total demise or oblivion to posterity.

Mindful of this, in September 1991, I made a proposal to Ken Saro-Wiwa to the effect that we should make a major documentation of the *Yaa* tradition based on my research on the subject matter. He was very optimistic about the proposal after reading my papers on the subject matter. At that time, he had just completed work on Ogoni folk tales and was considering the possibility of documenting Ogoni proverbs. He saw that a combination of my work and his work on the folk tales and the proverbs would give us a full picture of Ogoni world-view and culture, and would therefore form the basis for a literary documentation. So he wrote back to say, among other things, "Your work, the folk tales and the proverbs together will prepare the way for a possible novel ... Let us pray for life and the gift of the gods"[11] While this dream was being masterminded, within a brief space of time, the crisis and the tragedy which provided a basis for his judicial murder, struck. His untimely death was therefore a serious setback.[12]

The idea was to produce a type of historical novel or a literary work in which the dumb characters described in my work would be made to speak, act, and voice out the things, episodes, and events described. We would like to invite other writers, artists, and intellectuals to come forward to take up this challenge. We believe that the *Yaa* tradition is a suitable material for such a literary documentation. it is interesting, educative, progressive, creative, dramatic, historical, original, indigenous, unique, exuberant and colourful. Such a useful piece of culture should not be allowed to disappear. Instead, effort should be made to adapt it into our educational system as part of the creative art of humanity.

If this is done, it would act as a useful material for character formation in our youths by its discipline, by discouraging anti-social behaviours, such as theft, murder, drug abuse, secret cultism, sorcery, perverse sexual behaviours, indolence, truancy, and disrespect to elders. Instead, it would inculcate a positive attitude to life by inducing a desire for hard work, excellence, creativity and respect for human dignity and the sanctity of life.

Economic Activities

Ogoniland is a fertile plateau rising to about 100 ft above sea level. From very early beginnings agriculture had been their chief occupation, with yams as the principal crop. Other occupations such as palm wine tapping, palm fruit cutting, long-distance trade and fishing, were special occupations for which selected individuals were trained.

By the sixteenth and seventeenth centuries, yam cultivation had become a competitive occupation attracting classified chiefly titles for the best and most successful farmers.[13] This period also marked the rising tide of the trans-Atlantic slave trade; and large quantities of yams were being exported because it was the principal staple food used in feeding the slaves during their journey across the Atlantic. The class of titled yam chiefs controlled agriculture and yam production. They produced yams both for export and for home consumption. They established a yam club (*piá zia*), a yam house (*to zia*), and a yam shrine (*si zia*), in every village, manned by a yam priest (*te-zia*). They gathered at the yam house for two Ogoni weeks (ten days) every year to perform rituals and sacrifices before the start of every farming season.

The class of titled chiefs gradually became the owners of the largest farms in some of the best farming areas of the communities. Because of their wealth people who owned land, who were in financial need, pledged their farms to them for a loan of money. As a result of this process coupled with the high density of the population, agricultural land became a scarce commodity in Ogoni. Moreover, as evidence of wealth and social status, and as part of the requirement for the award of titles, this class of chiefs were required to marry a number of foreign (i.e. extra-ethnic or inter-ethnic) wives in addition to their local ones. This necessitated the appointment of agents from the class of long-distance traders, who secured such wives from the Igbo and Ibibio hinterlands via the Imo or Cross River waterways. This type of marriage became a status symbol in social circles and in relationships. The rhetoric question was often asked *O bee yae gbŏ?* ("Did you buy a slave?"), or *O yae gbŏ ni?* ("You bought a slave eh?"). These queries were often spoken with stern rebuff or show off, accompanied with a twitch of the face, eyes, and voice. The implication was that wives married from such far away places, were generally docile and more loyal than their local counterparts. Hence the above was a natural re-action of persons, who felt that they had a measure of autonomy, independence, or rights, which should not be interfered with. Because the yam chiefs were very hardworking and had accumulated much wealth, they earned chiefly titles, married many wives and established their own House (*Be*), which became political units of society. It will be seen that it was this class of men who were able to put their sons forward to perform the *yaagĕ* tradition. It will be seen also that it was from this class of men that those who performed the *yaawĩi* (rite of sons) tradition emerged. Viewed from another angle, it will be seen also that *yaagĕ* was promoted by this social class because it ensured the perpetuation of their own class. This will be clear when we discover that the youths who performed the *yaagĕ* tradition also constituted the first social class of elites in Ogoni society.

3. The Family System

There has been no anthropological study of Ogoni kinship system and culture. Consequently, there is not in existence any systematic classification of Ogoni family system and mode of inheritance. Although the Ogoni system deserves such a systematic study, unfortunately, this writer is not a professional anthropologist. it is likely, therefore, that the use of terms in this section will be inadequate. Nevertheless, the main concern here is to historically explain the changes that had taken place in Ogoni family system since the sixteenth century until the present, which have had some impact on the *yaa* tradition.

Evidence from oral tradition and extrapolations from the beginning of the last century, indicates that the family system in Ogoniland has undergone some radical changes. Before the seventeenth century, marriage in Ogoni was based on endogamous matrilineal system. As I have explained elsewhere, the first ruler of Ogoni was a woman by name Kwaanwaa. After the death of Kwaanwaa at Gure, the succession did not pass to her son but to her first and only daughter, Za. After the death of Za, succession also passed to her own first daughter by name Bariyaayoo, who ruled at Luawii. After Bariyaayoo, the succession went to another daughter, a great grand daughter of Za by name Gbeneyaana, whose seat of rulership was at Ka-Gwaara. The last of these royal ancestresses was Gbenebeka, who succeeded on the Ka-Gwaara stool in the sixteenth century. It is the name of Gbenebeka that is mentioned in the Colonial

Intelligence Reports:

> Mr. Jeffreys refers in detail to a belief in a common ancestress of Divine origin, Gbenebeka, but I am unable to confirm the fact that this belief is universal among all the clans of the tribe. At the same time, there can be little doubt that the name Gbenebeka is one of very great significance, and her shrine at Gwaara possesses even to day a very real importance as being the most important place of sacrifice throughout the conutry.[16]

This shows clearly that the early Ogoni kinship system was matrilineal. However, by the sixteenth century, the marriage system in Ogoni had changed from matrilineal endogamous to patrilineal exogamous. Several factors contributed to the early change in Ogoni kinship system. The most important was the practice of marrying foreign wives by wealthy men as a requirement when they took titles, whether war titles or yam titles. Another factor was the insecurity suffered by women during periods of crisis. For example in the sixteenth century, during the civil war known as the "Baan Wars", many non-indigenous wives who lived closer to their husbands, were better protected. Moreover, the wealthy men desired to have their own heirs, who would inherit their estate. This desire was partly satisfied by the children begotten from their foreign wives. Consequently, some of the indigenous wives and their children also demanded their rights in their husbands and father's estate. Early in the last century, Daryll Forde noticed the beginning of a similar development among the Yako.[17] These factors actualized and stimulated the early change from matrilineal to patrilineal virilocal system of marriage in Ogoniland. As to why this change took place among the Ogoni before the other ethnic groups in the rest of the Niger Delta, is that the economic determinism first occurred among the Ogoni before the rest of the Delta.[18]

4. Mode of Inheritance

Before the sixteenth century, i.e. during the period of matrilineal succession, inheritance also went to the first born daughter (*sira*). A lesser part was distributed among the other daughters. What the daughters inherited included things like cloths, household property, domestic animals, equipment, farms, plantain groves, money, office, coconut trees, other fruit trees etc. Mother's brothers took charge of raffia palm and oil palm bushes. The sons inherited nothing directly from their blood mothers and nothing from their blood fathers.[19] When they were grown up and had been trained by their maternal uncles and, perhaps had become fathers themselves, they began to inherit the raffia palm and oil palm bushes, which were under the charge of their mother's brothers, as the latter grew older.

By the sixteenth century, when Ogoni changed to patrilineal virilocal system, the mode of inheritance also changed radically. By that time, wealthy titled men had established their own autonomous Houses (*Be*). Their wives and children lived with them in their own compounds or Houses. At the death of such a man, his first-born son (*saaro*) succeeded him as head of the House, and he inherited the bulk of his father's wealth. Part of this wealth was however, distributed among the first-sons of other wives. The first-born son (Saaro) in this context means the first son of the first wife. The daughters inherited the property of their mothers, the bulk of which went to the first-born daughters. As noted above, the first daughters were not married out. The other daughters were married out; and they moved to their husbands homes.

With the foregoing analysis, we hope that we have done our best to present a bird's-eye-view of the environment and background of the *yaa* tradition. Our expectation is that this will go a long way to aid the understanding of the reader. However, before we proceed to the *yaa* tradition itself, we would like to define a few of the terms used explicitly or implicitly in this book, in order to dispel any possible ambiguity from the mind of the reader.

5. Definition of Terms

In this book, the word patrilineage (*gà*) is used to refer to the father's line of kins. It refers to the lineage of the legitimate father and, to that extent, it excludes all illegitimate fathers, such as a father by adultery, by concubinage, or by the old matrilineal connection. All such fathers are called *tegboo*, meaning "father-outside-the-gate". They are not legal fathers because they did not marry the mothers and did not pay the recognized bridewealth. In short, they lacked status as legally admitted sons-in-law into the family circles of the women. Patrilineage in our context has a genealogical tree known as ga and a historical origin dating back to the fifteenth or sixteenth century, when wealthy, titled men began to establish autonomous families and Houses (*Be*) through long-distance marriages. The autonomous Houses (*Be*) were markedly ruled by a line of accredited successors or first-born sons called *Saaro*.

Similarly, in this book the term matrilineage (*Bua*) is used to refer to the mother's line of kins. It does not imply a notion of double descent, as practised among the Yako,[20] nor suggest membership of a localized lineage organisation or citizenship of a chiefdom in which a mother's lineage is legally domiciled, as among the Ashanti of southern Ghana.[21]

In our context, the term matrilineage now has a more religious or ritual undertone than political or economic. Its root is based on Ogoni's world-view and a belief that blood or essence passed from mother to children and with it the divine order of governance.[22] They believed that the Supreme Creator is feminine; and that although the world of nature was created, man was not created but born out of God's womb. God is therefore seen as the Great Mother (*Kawa Bari*) of mankind, from whom all authority and governance emanated.[23] This divine essence and authority had been passed on to the woman and was manifested in child-bearing. All mothers in turn, passed on this divine essence and authority to their daughters, particularly the first-born daughters. On the basis of this doctrine, during the matrilineal era, succession and inheritance passed to the first-born daughters.

A continuity or remnant of this doctrine can be seen in that after the transition to patrilineal system, the first born daughters were not married out. They remained in their father's houses, where they held the office of priestesses. Owing to the strong belief in a divine endowment of the matrilineal priestesses and the spiritual power they were believed to impart, pilgrimages were made to them during the performance of the *Yaa* tradition. Apart from these religious functions, no inheritance or any other obligations were involved.

Chapter Two

The Structure of Ogoni Society

1. Early Society

Several evidence indicate that quite early in their history, the Ogoni adopted youth training as a fundamental aspect of social organization. There are instances in the oral tradition where children born into the society were observed from childhood until they became responsible leaders of the society. An analysis of the social system of the early Ogoni society indicate that they had a system of organization and training which enabled youths of ability to gain the necessary political and economic experience from the grassroots till they grew up to occupy positions of leadership in the society.

As a result, Ogoni society was structured into social classes and categories. Overshadowing the society was the class known as *piá bẹẹ buẽ* (the rulers), which comprised the *Gbenemene* (King or Paramount Ruler), *piá Kanẽe* (the elders), *piá Kabaari* (the chiefs), and *piá Zuguru* (the lieutenants). Below the class of *piá bẹẹ buẽ* was the general class known as *piá Kẽbuẽ* (the commoners or masses). Within this class of *piá Kẽbuẽ* were the following social categories:

(1) *piá gbára* - The elite or gentlemen

(2) *piá Kunẽ Nẽe* - Commoners or ordinary free men

(3) *piá Kporowa* - The unmarried poor

(4) *Zooro/gbõ* - The slaves

(5) *piá saa nẽe* - The strangers

From the above we noticed that the social category called *piá ghara* or gentlemen were the closest to the class of *piá beẹ buẽ* (rulers). As a matter of fact, it was from the ranks of *piá gbára* that candidates for the class of *piá beẹ buẽ* were recruited. The question then arises, who were the *piá gbára* in Ogoni society? How did they attain their distinction? We shall answer these questions by a study of the *yaa* tradition, the institution from which the young men who constituted the social class of *piá gbára* were organized and produced.

The title *piá gbára* was the first social title in Ogoni which applied to every young man who had performed or undergone the traditional training and discipline called *yaagẽ*. The term means the rite of bearing arms. This is explained by the suffix 'gẽ' which means sword or matchet. Accordingly, a man or a youth who had performed the *yaagẽ* tradition was by custom allowed to wear an insignia publicly at any time. This was a short decorated two edged sword called *kọbẹgẽ* which was packed in a sheath and worn on the waist by a leather belt. The *kọbẹgẽ* served a dual purpose, both as a weapon and as the insignia of the bearer's social status. All the young men from adolescence to full adult were expected to undergo the *yaagẽ* traditional training before they were recognized in society. In later years, boys below early adulthood have been initiated because parents became anxious to have their sons perform the tradition while they were still alive. This assured them that their sons would not lapse into the lower social class called *kunẽ nẽe* (commoners or ordinary citizens).

2. Class Discriminations

The advantage was that persons who did not undergo the *yaagĕ* traditional training and experience were said to be physically and spiritually deficient, inactive and unwise (i.e. stupid in their spirit life).[24] They were therefore considered incapable of leadership or to speak for or represent others. For the same reasons they were not listed as fighting men for the community or as soldiers in time of war, because it was believed that in time of emergency, a warrior's spiritual soundness was vital. They believed that a spiritually weak person could easily be led astray and entrapped by the enemy. Since the *kunĕ nĕe* lacked the benefits gained from both the physical and the spiritual discipline, as well as the military experience which, the *yaagĕ* tradition provided, they were considered lacking in the essential qualities which equipped a man to fit well in an active society.

Moreover, the *kunĕ nĕe*, i.e. the man who had not performed the *yaagĕ* tradition, has vital political limitations. He could not take part in a political debate or deliberations. According to chief Nii:

> If an important matter occurred in the community and they wanted people to meet to discuss it, only those who had performed the *yaagĕ* tradition could enter the house where the matter was being discussed. Those who had not performed the *yaagĕ* tradition would sit outside and listen from outside. They could not be able to take part in the discussions.[25]

And Prince Tedee tells us that such persons were restricted from entering certain public places in the town.[26] Since eligibility was by no other qualification except the ability to pay the cost and the fact that the candidate must be a free citizen, the *yaagĕ* tradition might be seen, therefore, as an effective primary means of social stratification.

The impact of these social restrictions has continued into the present among persons above fifty years old, who knew the political, social and spiritual implications of the *yaa* tradition, even though the tradition itself was no longer being performed. For example, in December 1999, Peace Gospel International Church performed water baptism in Kono Boue Community in Khana Local Government Area of Rivers State. As the Pastor of the Church, I led the congregation to the community's principal stream called *Maawaabogo*. On reaching the stream, two elderly men and an elderly woman among the group refused to go into the water for the baptism. The entire congregation was shocked beyond comprehension, wondering why these persons should withdraw at the very last minute. Later the men and the woman confided to me that they had not performed the *yaa* tradition and that they withdrew because the stream was forbidden to them. They insisted that it was a high risk for them to contravene the traditional injunction. They however, agreed to be baptized if the venue of the baptism was changed. The next occasion, which was in April 2000, the woman and the two men got baptized because I took them to another stream called *Deepip* which was free for all citizens to bath in.

From the above personal experience, which happened recently, one could readily understand the strong influence the *yaa* tradition had on the political and social structure of Ogoni society in the by-gone years and centuries.

Fortunately or unfortunately, however, these restrictions are no longer being observed among the younger generations. The reason is that the *yaa* tradition is no longer being performed. And even, when it is performed, it is only a token performance and not as rigorous as tradition demanded. This was the case of chief Tax Kue of Boue, earlier referred to above, who did a token performance in 2001 in order to obtain a legal membership of the House Traditional Rulers of Boue as an elder. Such token performances do not produce anything near the degree of social and political effect which the actual performances used to produce on the society.

Chapter Three

The Yaagẽ Tradition

1. Youth Recruitment and Training

The *yaagẽ* tradition was not performed by youths exclusively. The youths performed the tradition under a rich, wealthy, and charismatic leader. This began when such a leader had declared his intention to perform they *yaawĩi* (rite of sons) tradition, in order to earn the title of *kabaari* (chief), as the leader or commander of a fighting force for his town or community.

The term *yaawĩi* is a combination of two words *yaa*, which means a "rite" and *wĩi*, which means a "child". Hence *yaawĩi* means the rite of raising sons or warriors. Consequently, the man performing the *yaawĩi* tradition must by custom be a person who possessed good leadership qualities and unblemished character. He must also be a good fighter and a charismatic leader. These qualities in addition to his wealth, guaranteed the approval of his proposal by the Elders and inspired the confidence of parents to entrust their sons to him for training in the performance of the *yaagẽ* tradition.

Once such a man had received the go-ahead from the elders, parents from all parts of the district brought their sons to enrol under him in order for them to perform the *yaagẽ* tradition. From that moment on the man began to be known and addressed by all as the *tẹ-yaa* (*yaa* father), and the youths so enrolled under him became known as *piá dam yaa* (the *yaa* masculines or males). Besides, each *yaa* male or man was allowed to choose two men from his community who had previously performed the *yaagẽ* tradition, who were appointed as his *tẹ be* (house fathers). The choice of the house fathers was the responsibility of the *dam yaa*'s parents. These men became the day-to-day companions and trainers of the *dam yaa* throughout the period of the performance, which lasted for about two years.

2. Pilgrimages to Ancestral Homes (*Si Bu Zim*)

After the registration of the youths, the first series of activities consisted of performances called *si bu zim* which comprised a formal homage or pilgrimage to the ancestral shrines of the *tẹ yaa*'s ancestors.

The first, called *si bu zim tẹ* (pilgrimage to the sacred shrines of the patrilineage ancestors), took place at the patriarchal compound of the *tẹ-yaa*, i.e. at the compound of the founder of his patrilineage. All the chiefs, elders, and the principal men of the district were invited to this occasion. Goats and fowls were slaughtered for meat and plenty of food and drinks were served throughout the day. Many sacrifices and rituals were performed and libations poured to the ancestors. One of the features of this occasion was the presentation of cash gifts (*waara zim*) to each of the titled patriarchs or first-born sons (*saro*) of the patrilineage (*gã*), as their names were recited from the earliest of them to the most recent. According to Chief Kiriki, the cash gifts varied from three to four new manilas (*ãa kpugi*) each. Without this formal way of informing the ancestors about the title taking, tragedy could occur which could terminate the whole project. The aim of the *tẹ-yaa* was to prevent any natural or supernatural interruption, such as sickness, accident or death, happening to any of the candidates. Any such tragedy was blamed on the *te-yaa*'s inability naturally or supernaturally. For that reason, all the *yaa* men (*dam yaa*) were required to be present on such occasions, in order to benefit from he rituals and the activities of the ceremonies.

As a requirement for their participation, each *yaa* man was required to pay a prescribed fee towards the cost of the rituals and the activities. For this occasion, the traditional fee paid by each *dam yaa* was four manilas and seven large yams. Where the *dam yaa* was a first-born son (*saro*), the fee was thrice the prescribed amount, plus seven large yams. A second-born son (*la*) paid twice the prescribed amount, plus seven yams. Where all three or more sons of one family were performing the tradition, the payment by the last-born son was waived. This was a type of traditional rebate or discount in favour of such a family.

The second homage or pilgrimage called *si bu zim ka*, (homage to matriarchal shrine) was made to the *te-yaa*'s matriarchal house (*bua*). In preparation for this occasion, the *te-yaa* sent money in advance to the head of the matrilineage house for them to make ready all food and drinks for the entertainment of the guests. On the appointed date, all the chiefs and principal men of the district and all the members of the matrilineage, gathered at the matriarchal house. As on the previous occasion, rites, rituals and libations were performed amidst a great reunion of kindreds and peoples.

As at the patrilineage, cash gifts (*waara zim*) were also presented to all the matriarchs or first-born daughters (*sira*) of the matrilineage. Their names were recited starting from the earliest to the latest. As on the previous occasion, all the *yaa* men were required to take part and to pay the prescribed fees, following the pattern described above.

Next, the *tẹ-yaa* visited all the important places in Ogoniland to perform the traditional rites and to pay the prescribed fees. Among such places were the houses of the founders of the component towns, the war shrines and the matriarchal house of Gbenebeka at Ka-Gwaara, the last of the early female ancestresses and the universal rulers of Ogoniland.

Finally, the *tẹ-yaa* went to his ancient matrilineage or the house of his great, great grandmother (*si buzim nama kaama*) to perform the rites and to pay the prescribed fees. As usual, he sent money in advance in preparation for the occasion. On the appointed date, the ceremonies proceeded as at the matrilineage. The climax of the ceremonies on this occasion was a holy bath or baptism performed on the *tẹ-yaa* by the priestess of the ancient matriarchal house. This baptism was supposed to give him his greatest spiritual fortification and insulation against external negative forces and to endow him with wisdom, intelligence and a sense of direction in the spirit world which, according to the elders, was the basis of proper conduct, success, and right actions in the natural world.

While the *tẹ-yaa* was performing the above traditional actions, the *yaa* men also went to their different patrilineage and matrilineage houses to perform similar ceremonies and rituals and to pay the prescribed fees. But theirs was private and low keyed. Nonetheless, it served the important purpose of giving formal notice to kindred relations about their participation in the on-going *yaagẽ* performance.

All these pilgrimages, especially those by the *tẹ-yaa* were not an easy-going matter, nor were they accomplished within a predetermined time frame. Each of them was preceded by intense diplomatic activity. Emissaries were sent back and forth, issues were raised, past disagreements were settled, matters of grievances and wrongdoings, were raked up and dealt with, contradictions were clarified, new matters and questions were raised and properly dealt with. In short all such matters were properly taken care of behind the scenes before the actual date for each pilgrimage was announced. As the pilgrimages extended to farther away strategic places like Ka-Gwaara, the sphere of diplomatic activity also widened to include matters of inter-clan, inter-community and inter-chiefdom relations. Thus all such matters were taken up and dealt with in order to ensure an atmosphere of complete peace throughout the period of the *yaawĩi* and *yaagẽ* traditional performances. Where such matters were overlooked and the peace was broken, the performance was said to have been a failure. And if the disturbance was severe the entire performance could be terminated midway before completion. This was the reason for the intense diplomatic activity to make sure that all hands were on deck for a successful completion of the performance.

Meanwhile, the cost of all these diplomatic activities rested on the shoulders of the *te-yaa*. However, in the final analysis, the *te-yaa* also received an overflow of income in the form of money and goods brought by the endless visitors to the occasion, including chiefs, elders, principal men from far and near throughout Ogoniland, who came with wine, money, and gifts to show their solidarity and support for his achievement and to declare their approval for his successful performance of the noble tradition. Thus at the end of the performance, the *te-yaa* usually became richer, wealthier and more famous than when he began.

Chapter Four

Field Activities

1. Social Interactions

After the ceremonies and rites at the patriarchal and at the matriarchal houses and the diplomatic activities at various strategic levels throughout the nationality, the traditional performance moved full swing into the field stage. This began with a traditional banquet called *atãadee geere* at the compound of the *te-yaa*. This was really a huge open-air picnic by the *yaa* men. Each *yaa* man or *dam yaa*, was accompanied by his *te be* (house fathers). By custom they were required to bring along a cock, a hen, yams, plantains, palm wine. Pots, condiments and wood. They set up their cooking positions on both sides of the broad street leading from the compound of the *te-yaa*, forming two rows of cooking extending as far as possible into the adjacent streets. There was a wide space in-between for people to pass through. The banquet began from about 5 p.m. and continued into the night.

To secure choice positions, participants came earlier in the day to plant a wild cocoyam plant (*Colocasia antiquorum*) at the position of their choice. Once that was done, no one else occupied that position. It is significant to notice that the name *atãadee geere* had evolved from the rows of wild cocoyam plants which lined the streets used for the banquet. The name comprises several component words viz., *atãa*, which means a "row", *dee* which means a "road", or street, and *geere* which means "cocoyam" (i.e. old cocoyam), meaning the feast of a "road lined with cocoyams".

One of the aims of the banquet was to foster a sense of brotherhood and friendship among the *yaa* men. Other young men who had previously performed the tradition came to partake in the festivities. Men who had not performed the tradition were forbidden to eat the dinner. According to the elders, if any such a person ate the dinner, the person died within days. In recent years, several youths and men who had not performed the tradition have been reported dead after eating the dinner.

Each *yaa* man gave a share of his dinner to the *tẹ-yaa*. According to Chief Kiriki, each *yaa* man gave one chicken leg, two yams and the upper segment of the plantain bunch to the *yaa* father. The latter in turn shared his collections with the chiefs and elders of the town in the following morning.

After the banquet, all the *yaa* men withdrew from public appearances and from their parents and relatives and retired into a groom confinement called *bọgọ-yaa*. Their mothers were forbidden to see them. This lasted for about three weeks (*taa eeri*). During this period they underwent a spiritual rebirth and holiness. Consequently, they were not supposed to have any physical contacts with women. Men who had slept with women the night before, were forbidden to come into their presence. A phenomenon called *pà yaa* was believed to issue from their bodies and cling to any female who came into physical contact with them. The *pà yaa* was said to have undesirable and unpleasant consequences for such a woman, unless a ritual or sacrifice was performed to 'remove' it.

The *yaa* men remained with their house fathers (*tẹ-be*) and ate only the food provided by them. They could, however, associate among themselves. A virgin boy or a page called *giã yaa* was attached to each *yaa* man and he acted as his messenger. When the *yaa* man moved to any place, the *giã yaa* accompanied him carrying his carved stool called *tã yaa* for him to sit on. The *dam yaa* was not supposed to sit on a common seat during this period of personal holiness. They slept on special mats called *bui yaa* and kept their skins smooth and fresh by regularly rubbing at bed time a skin-toning preparation called *do*, which they washed off in the mornings. Among the instructions which the *yaa* men received during the performance of the tradition are the following:

1. that they should regard their bodies as holy. Accordingly, they were expected to live a disciplined life, especially with respect to food, drinks, sex, and material things.
2. that in spirit-life the *yaa* men had taken precedence over or superseded persons who had not performed the tradition, irrespective of age.
3. that the *yaa* men had become leaders. They were therefore not supposed to take advice or instructions from persons who had not performed the tradition or let themselves to be led by them.
4. that leadership by non-performers was contrary to the divine order of things.
5. that the *yaa* men were spiritually wiser and stronger than any one else who had not performed the tradition.

6. that proper conduct in spirit-life was the basis of success in the natural world.

Throughout the period of the initiation, which lasted for about two years, the *yaa* men also received instructions in the art of swordsmanship or fencing, in the leading occupations, such as yam cultivation, tree climbing, palm wine tapping, oil palm cutting, and instructions in traditional music, art, and sports. In this way, the *yaa* men became imbued with a high degree of self-confidence, a positive attitude to life and a sense of mission or leadership to their communities.

2. **Presentation to the *Yaa* Totem (*Si Yo-uwe Yaa*)**
At the end of the groom confinement, all the *yaa* men and their house fathers (*tẹ be*) dressed in fine cloths with bells on their waists, assembled at the compound of the *tẹ yaa* (*yaa* father).

They were all dressed in traditional pageantry with each man bearing an iron weapon called *egà yaa*. This was a long pointed iron shaft, which was borne on the left shoulder with its pointed end knobbed and held high. Presumably, this was the type of iron weapon first used by the Ogoni ancestors. Accompanied by the elders and all the principal men of the district, they proceeded in a gorgeous processional parade through the important streets of the town being led by an ancient dancing club called *sóosó* amidst great cheering by crowds of admirers, parents, relatives, well-wishers and friends. This was the occasion on which the *tẹ-yaa* and his *yaa* men presented themselves before the *yaa* totem or deity known as *ku* or *yọ-uwe yaa*.

The main requirement on this occasion was a ritual offering. Each *yaa* man was required to present a live poppy dog to the *yo-uwe yaa* or *yaa* deity as a sacrificial offering. The *yaa* father (*tẹ-yaa*) sacrificed a lamb. He killed the lamb by boxing it with his fists. This was called *bog-pée* and it was supposed to give him a healthy long life.

Each *yaa* man presented himself before the *yo-uwe yaa* and received blessings. The priest of the *yaa* deity was assisted by a select group of elders. They smeared white chalk marks on each *dam yaa* while voicing some incantations or prayers. The white chalk marks were made on the right arm, on the forehead, on the chest, and a long one from the middle of the chest down to the navel. On the back part, the white chalk was made on the two shoulder blades, on the two sides of the back and a long one on the mid-rib from below the neck down to the waist. These white chalk markings were the symbols of the blessings which they had received. It is to be remembered that the *yaa* men were dressed in new bright cloths, smartly knotted on their waists, but their bodies were bare from waist up, so that their fresh, youthful bodies were fully exposed. Hence the white chalk marks on their bodies were clearly seen.

As each *yaa* man received his blessings from the presence of the deity, each returned joyfully to his home accompanied by his house fathers (*tẹ-be*). As they went, they gave gifts to various groups of people they met on the way, particularly groups of farm workers (*etǎa wii*), to groups of traders or market women (*etǎa du*), and to groups of domestic servants, such as water carriers (*etǎa mǎa*). It would seem that this aspect of the tradition was created to give practical expression to the generosity culture which was one of the pillars of the *yaa* tradition.

3. **The Mullet Banquet (*Egara Aka*)**

At the end of the *yọ-uwe-yaa* the *tẹ yaa* announced the date for another banquet. This was called *ègàra áká* (lit. scattering the mullets). The name probably derived from the principal dish at this banquet, which was mullet. According to Chief Kiriki, each *yaa* man or *dam yaa* was required to bring a specific number of mullets. A first-born son was required to bring sixty mullets plus one large fish namely a shark (*táe*), while a second-born son was required to bring fifty mullets and a shark. In addition, each *yaa* man also brought yams (usually seven), plantains and palm wine. As usual, the last-born of three or more sons of a family participating received free dinner.

On the appointed date all the *yaa men* and their house fathers assembled at the compound of the *yaa* father at about 5 p.m. Unlike the previous banquet, the cooking of this dinner was done centrally by attendants. the mullet banquet was another great occasion in the performance of the *yaagẹ́* tradition, featuring a great deal of sharing and fellowshipping by the *yaa* men. Other young men who had performed the tradition were all welcome to enjoy free dinner. As custom required, each *yaa* man gave a share of the fish to the *tẹ-yaa* and to the representatives of each of the ancient patrilineages present at the banquet. After the banquet, the *yaa* father fixed a date for a grand parade of himself and his lieutenants or *yaa* men through the main streets of the town. The occasion gave the tẹ-yaa the opportunity to give expression to his successful performance of the yaawĩi tradition. Chief Iyoro who himself performed the tradition in 1983, explains that the day of the parade was the day, the tẹ-yaa showed off to the public the fact that he has become one of the great leaders of the area. According to him, this was the occasion the yaa father dressed in his chiefly apparels, adorned with costly ornaments.[31]

The first place the parade visited was the local war shrine. The yaa father was accompanied in the parade by the chiefs and elders and by all the yaa men. They walked in a grand procession through the major streets of the town and visited the important places and centres. All along the routes the tẹ-yaa constantly dipped his hand into his purse and scattered[32] handfuls of cash to the cheering crowds of admirers. Similarly, when the parade approached an important road junction or the gate of a chief or titled man, the guards barricaded the way and demanded payment of tolls. Whenever this was done, the tẹ-yaa dipped his hand into his purse and gave them money. As soon as money was paid, the barricades were quickly removed and the procession continued until all the important places and streets had been covered.

4. **The Holy Bath or Baptism**

After the parade, the traditional performance entered its last lap. The yaa father then sent money to the house of pẹẹ, an ancient musical society to hire them to play for him and his yaa men. Meanwhile he has fixed a date for a holy baptism of his lieutenants or *yaa* men. The evening before this baptismal ritual, each *yaa* man slept alone in the house of his senior patron or house father (*te-be*). About 4.30 a.m. in the following morning, each *yaa* father (*te-be*) took his *yaa* man to the nearest running stream for a holy bath or baptism. This was a running bath.

Led by the house father the *dam yaa* dipped his feet into the water and ran away as fast as he could towards the village or town. As soon as he caught a glimpse of the village, he turned and ran to dip his feet into the stream again. He repeated this until seven times. At the seventh time,[33] he threw himself into the water and took a smart quick bath and ran out of the water straight to the home of his house father from where he set out. The whole bath must be completed before twilight, and no fly[34] must perch on his body during the ritual.

All the while, the house father was running with him and keeping the count until the seventh time. The *yaa* man must be completely nude,[35] his cloth being held by the house father. At the seventh time when the *dam yaa* throws himself into the water, the house father left him and ran home with the *dam yaa*'s cloth. In that way, the *dam yaa* had no choice but to run home nude and alone. This ritual was called *su bete* (snatching away cloth from another's loin). He stayed that way at the home of his house father until about 8 p.m. the next night when the "separation dance" "*yep pee*" commenced.

5. The Separation Dance (*Yep Pee*)

There were two musical societies. One was called the elders' *pee* (*pee piá kanĕe*). This *pee* was sacred and was played for honourable men. Young men who were virgins were allowed to dance this *pẹẹ*. This dance took place at night, starting from about 8.00 p.m. at the palace of the founder and paramount chief of the town, who is also the patron of the elders' *pẹẹ*. The musicians played inside the palace while the *yaa* men gathered outside from where each *yaa* man danced in turn to the music. They danced one by one from outside into the palace, where the elders were seated and placed their hands on a sacred instrument and then danced from there to the outside where a crowd of spectators, friends, and well-wishers were gathered, amidst great cheering and applause.

The second *pẹe* which took place at a separate location, was called *pẹẹ izā*. This *pẹe* was not sacred; it was open to all men who had lost their holiness. According to Chief Iyoro, the *izā* were men who could not keep themselves holy, such as men who had extra-marital sex or carnal relations with a twin mother, or with a strange woman, and boys who had had sex before performing the *yaagē* tradition. Chief Nwilabba explains that youths of this category were dubbed *èlọ* (deviants), and were eliminated from the society or sold into slavery.[36] According to another informant, if such a youth concealed the truth and danced the holy *pẹe* and touched the sacred instrument, he dropped dead instantly.[37]

It is evident that the *yaage* tradition had within it a machinery meant to purge society of such deviant youths. This explains why at certain stages in the traditional performances, parents, especially mothers were forbidden to see their sons. This in effect was a method of conditioning the would-be unlucky mothers for such an eventuality. Meanwhile the virgin *yaa* men who danced the holy *pẹe* were acclaimed successful, and were received with great joy by their parents and sponsors. Gifts and presents were made to them by parents, relatives, friends and well-wishers.

It is to be noted that some of the men who danced the unholy *pẹe* i.e. the *pẹe-izā* were men who had no opportunity to perform the *yaage* tradition when they were youths because of lack of sponsors, either because their parents were too poor to sponsor them or that their parents died early before they were due to perform. Some of such men later sponsored themselves through their own self effort and industry. *Yaa* men of this category were also highly praised and applauded because of their hard work and determination in life. Gifts and presents were made to them by well-wishers and friends in the same way as to the virgin youths even though they did not dance the holy *pẹe* nude because of their age.

6. **The *Yaa* Marathon (*Teerà Yaa*)**

Finally, about 5 a.m. the following morning, the *yaa* marathon began. The race, which was non-gregarious and non-competitive began with the *izā* men, that is those who danced the unholy *pẹe*. They wore around their waists a mini raffia cloth called *ígwà*. They began the race early in order to cover the local areas when most people especially the women and girls, were not awake to line the routes.

The virgin *yaa* men began theirs about six o'clock in the morning. They ran theirs almost nude. On their waist they wore a leather girdle to which was attached a bronze figure called *gēe-yaa*. On their heads was a circular crown called *giē-yaa* with a strap passed under the chin to keep it in place. To the crown was attached one or two eagle fathers. Each *yaa* man was armed with two short curved swords called *Kọbẹgē*, one in hand and the other on the waist packed in a sheath and held by a leather belt.

Each *yaa* man ran between two guards, the house fathers, who wore their cloths knotted, gathered, and tucked. The *yaa* man's page (*giã yaa*) wore a leather girdle with the bronze figure attached and carried the *yaa* man's carved stool (*tã yaa*) in one hand and sword in the other.

Dressed in this way each *yaa* party marched to the compound of the *tẹ-yaa*. There in the open court, each *yaa* man stood on his mat (*buí-yaa*) ready to start the race. When everything was set, the *dam yaa*'s virgin sister and first-born daughter or priestess of his father's house (*sira*), came forward carrying a little bowl of oil-chop made from *gẹẹrẹ* (old cocoyam) and put a sop of the stuff into the *dam yaa*'s mouth. As soon as the sop[38] entered his mouth, the 'warrior' set off with his guards and page; the guards or house fathers running slightly abreast him, one on either side and his page running behind. As they ran they followed specific routes through the towns and communities and only stopped briefly at important places.

The *yaa* marathon marked the climax of the *yaagē* traditional performance. All along the routes were crowds of people, especially women and girls, who cheered with great enthusiasm at the sight of so many young men taking part in this traditional exercise. As the race progressed, the public made comments on the individual runners. Characteristics such as fastness, trim-figure, brave looks, etc. attracted favourable comments. Other characteristics such as plump provided vents for light-heartedness and joy. The two guards or patrons protected the *dam yaa* and gave him direction at appropriate points along the routes.

As the race moved from the local areas into the neighbouring towns and communities, the exercise became truly war-like. People in those places attempted to snatch the eagle from the *dam yaa*'s crown. In such circumstances, the guards and the *dam yaa* brandished their swords and forced their way to safety. According to tradition, if the *dam yaa*'s eagle was taken, that was tantamount to taking the warrior prisoner. In such circumstances, the guards negotiated to recover the eagle by paying a ransom before the race continued again.

At certain friendly places, they rested briefly, during which the *dam yaa* sat on his carved stool. Throughout the race each *yaa* party kept chewing a certain watery plant called *àting* (*Castus afer*) in order to prevent exhaustion, husky voice, or dry throat. This was necessary because, as they ran, they kept voicing certain words intermittently punctuated with loud shouts and yululations, as shown in this illustration.

Leader	Tow	Tow
Response	whoa	whoa
Leader	Tow	Tow
Response	whoa	whoa
Leader	Tow	Tow
Response	whoa	whoa
Leader	Tow	Tow
Response	whoa	whoa

Yaa rhythm/chorus

The race ended at about 5 o'clock in the evening with a traditional cutting down of a plantain plant at the outskirts of the town. The plantain plant must be cut down with just one stroke of the *dam yaa*'s sword. In later periods when boys of younger age were initiated, the stem of the plantain plant was thinned to a suitable size. The custom of cutting the plantain plants was probably an act of war reminiscent of the execution of an enemy or prisoner of war. This is explained by the fact that it was done at the end of the race and on the outskirts of the town.

Early in the following morning, a simple ritual was performed on each *ḍam yaa* to remove the *pà yaa* from each of them. According to another informant, the *pà yaa* was a negative influence or spirit force which tended to cling to the *dam yaa* after the performance, having been attracted by the activities of the *yaa* tradition.[39] A special ritual was therefore performed to remove such influence and to banish them to the sea.

Without this ritual, the *dam yaa* would behave abnormally and might have constant nightmares. Prince Isaanee Nii[40] explains that a similar ritual was performed on warriors when they returned from battle before they were allowed to return to their families.

7. Tree Planting

Finally at the end of the whole performance, the *tẹ-yaa* was conferred with the title of *Kabaari* and was admitted to the ranks of rulers as a chief. His compound became classified as one of the notable compounds or Houses in Ogoni. As an insignia, a certain live tree variously called *té-Bàri* (tree of God) or té méne (tree of wealth) was planted in the centre of his compound. With that, his compound became recognized as one of the compounds to be visited by public processions, dances, outings, and masquerades. Moreover, the passage or road through the front of the compound became a tribute or toll collecting point during processions, public outings, or performances.

Chapter Five

Historical Origins Background and Impact

1. Origin of the Yaa Tradition

In chapter one, we traced the origin of the Ogoni ancestors to the ancient Ghana empire, the region of the headwaters of the great Niger river. Our investigation showed that the *Yaa* tradition was introduced at the initial settlement at Nama by the Ogoni founding ancestors. Based on Linguistic evidence, this initial settlement has been dated to as early as 15 B.C. This date corroborates with dates derived from written evidence by the Greek historian, Herodotus, and by Walter Rodney.

After a rigorous examination of the evidence, we came to the conclusion that the *Yaa* tradition was indeed part of a youth culture and training with which the Ogoni ancestors were familiar in their country of origin before they settled in their present domain. Our evidence showed that they left their former country in a period of great civil strife and became a wandering army under arms. Consequently, and as a matter of necessity, they held firmly to the *Yaa* tradition, which was a way of keeping their society and the youths constantly active for their own survival. This view of the origin of the *Yaa* tradition is strengthened by the fact that there is no evidence of cross-cultural transmission, as no similar tradition has been recorded among any of Ogoni's neighbours, and none yet elsewhere in Africa.

2. Economic and Environmental Determinism

The *Yaa* tradition, as the soul of Ogoni cultural heritage, could not have survived if the ancestors had settled in an impoverished environment. In such a situation they would have been forced to scatter or wander about seeking what to scrape off the soil in order to survive. Fortunately, Ogoniland was a fertile territory endowed with abundant water supply. Agriculture and fishing were well developed. Forest resources such as oil palms, raffia palms, and other economic trees were well tapped. They established a canoe industry at Ko on the Imo River, which became the major source of the product in the Eastern Niger Delta. Consequently, the Ogoni became the distributors of both small fishing canoes and the large transport canoes throughout the region.[41] They supplied their Ijo neighbours who depended very much on canoes but did not make canoes.[42]

They also established a large pot industry at Kono Bone, which supplied water pitchers and pots of various descriptions not only to their Ijo neighbours but also to their Igbo and Ibibio hinterland neighbours. The distribution of pots became an important aspect of long-distance trade using large canoes and providing jobs for a sizeable crop of men, who traversed the nooks and corners of the creek and rivers of the region. All these, in addition to yam cultivation and yam export, produced a class of wealthy men who began to use their money for acquiring social titles, marrying foreign and local wives and for promoting cultural activities such as the *Yaawĩi* tradition under which the *Yaagẽ* tradition for the training of the youths was performed. Thus economic well-being and social stability were very instrumental in promoting and sustaining the *Yaa* tradition. This was clearly evident in that those who were poor could not perform it, and because they could not perform it, they lacked status in society and lapsed as second-class citizens.

3. Innovative Influence on the Family System

The introduction of "foreign" or long-distance marriages into title taking brought about many radical changes into the Ogoni family system. First, it marked the beginning of a truly nuclear family system because for the first time, wives lived with their husbands in their husband's compounds. For the first time also, husbands and wives began to have children whom they could call their own and who lived with them in their own homes as their future heirs. This consciousness encouraged such men to plan for the future of their heirs. One of such planning was to enrol them and finance their participation in the *Yaagẽ* tradition. It was an innovation which set in motion a period of "high society" competition with multiplier effect on the family structure, as men struggled to acquire wealth in order to perform the necessary traditions that enhanced their social status.

The result on the matrilineage system was disintegration. Daughters, especially the middle ones who did not have direct succession and inheritance, moved away to live with the men they loved. Mother's brothers now demanded monetary payment at the marriage of their sisters and sisters' daughters, so that they could use the money in marrying foreign wives. Once a precedence was set, others followed , and so the change from matrilineal endogamous to partilineal exogamous virilocal marriage began in Ogoniland. The attention and care of mother's brothers was diverted from their sister's sons to their own children. Many of such neglected children had to work very hard to salvage themselves. Those who could not do so, or who had no opportunity to do so, lapsed to second class citizens.

Although we have dated these changes to the fifteenth and sixteenth centuries, in actual fact they began much earlier. Our choice of the later date is predicated on the need to utilize the dates of the written reports by the Portuguese and the Dutch travellers, who described the people, culture, language and economic activity in a large town which has now been identified as Ogoni.[43] Our view is that by the time the Portuguese and the Dutch made their contacts, the things they described were already the results of centuries of development.

From what we know of the history of the Niger Delta, it means that the changes that took place in Ogoni were centuries ahead of similar changes in the rest of the Niger Delta. As noted above, these changes included long-distance trade, the establishment of autonomous houses and families, the change from matrilineal to patrilineal virilocal system of marriage, etc.

I have shown elsewhere[44] that when similar changes started in other parts of the Niger Delta, they were the results of the trans-Atlantic slave trade, which can be dated from the seventeenth to the nineteenth centuries. But although the change in the marriage system started in the rest of the Niger Delta during that period, it is still continuing and very far from being stabilized. The implication then is that the Ogoni were previously in the vanguard of several innovative changes in the Niger Delta until colonial times when, as a result of Ogoni's long resistance to colonial rule, it had to suffer not only the effects of conquest but also the consequences of tardiness in the schemes of colonial development. Nonetheless, the recent environmental campaign by the Ogoni under the aegis of MOSOP, which has now swept across the whole Niger Delta and, indeed, the rest of Nigeria like a wild fire, was neither an accident nor a co-incidence but an event reminiscent of the history and character of the region.

4. **Impact on the Social and Political Structure**

In most African Societies, such as among the Igbo, the Ijŏ, the Ibibio, or the Yako of the middle Cross River, age is the main determining factor in social classification. In such places, the society is divided into age-sets, and political power is vested in the oldest age set. In Ogoni, age is not a determinant of political power. A person could be old and yet has no political power. The determinant of social classes and political power for both sexes was the *Yaa* tradition.

The *Yaa* tradition prepares a young man for leadership and for life. By its teachings and discipline it inculcates an attitude of hard work, self-discipline, integrity, creativity, sound morality respect for the sanctity of the human spirit and the human worth, an attitude of generosity, friendship and good character. Your house-fathers were not only your teachers but they were also your model and companion. They took you daily to the farms and to the palm wine camps (*nuloo*), where at certain times of the day, elderly and experienced men retired to relax from their work. There you listened to them as they talked about almost everything under the sun.

They talked about sea travel, how one could come out of one's house at night and look into the sky and know whether there would be a storm at sea for the next two weeks, or whether it would be safe to cross a certain sea at a certain period of the day or night. They talked about how to look at the shape and position of the moon and know whether the fishermen would make a good catch during the week, or whether they would make no catch during the next two weeks. They talked about how to study the flight of birds and know whether a storm was imminent. They talked about the behaviour of animals at different times of the day and night, and at different times of the month and in different seasons. They talked about how to detect the footprints of animals and know the type of animal.

You listened to experts composed songs and oral poetry and discussed good 'prose' or oratory. They spoke idioms, proverbs and metaphors about various subjects and contexts. And, being protected by the convention that anything spoken at the *nuloo* (palm wine camp) could not be contested in law and the speaker could not be sued, they freely composed satires about the behaviours of certain individuals in certain situations and laughed heartily about the subjects. They discussed politics, economics and love. They discussed biographies and talked about certain great warriors or medicine men, how they behaved and what they did in certain emergencies. They demonstrated the different ways of using a tool or weapon. They showed you how to identify a raffia palm that would mature in the next two or three months. They showed where you tapped a matured raffia palm tree and it yielded the full amount of its sweet juices and where you tapped it and you got only a trickle.

These experiences continued almost on daily basis until you completed the *Yaagē* tradition. By the end of it, you knew you had learned a lot of things and that you could do so many things. You behaved in a certain respectable way with self-confidence and self-assurance. Moreover, during the training if a certain youth was found to be budding genius, without himself knowing it, information about him was passed on to the elders and to the authorities of the appropriate secret societies or clubs, where his talents would be properly utilized. And before long, he was discreetly lured or encouraged to become a member or associate member, regardless of his age. Each time the *Yaagē* tradition was performed, a number of such gifted youths were identified and they became the foremost leaders in their generation. others also became leaders according to their talents and abilities in the various occupations. Thus, it can be seen that the *Yaa* tradition was a special institution which had within it a mechanism that stratified Ogoni society. Accordingly, those youths who, because of poverty their parents could not sponsor them, did not have the opportunity to learn these things. They became ignorant of many practical things of life; their ability to perform in life was therefore limited. Thus, they naturally lapsed into the lower classes of society.

Similarly, the feminine *Yaa* tradition produced the same social class distinctions among the women folk. The feminine

Yaa tradition was very simple. The young women were not enrolled formerly under a *Yaa* mother or matron like the boys. But at the pre-marital age, they were organized into groom clubs known as *Bogonðo* or *Koo*. During this period, which lasted for about two years or more, they were restrained from engaging in strenuous farm work but they performed the light domestic tasks. Each of these groom clubs was under the supervision of two women, who instructed them on many practical things of life, including how to take care of themselves as future wives and mothers.

The girls dressed in long, baggy raffia gowns, which covered them from top to the ankles. The girls were not supposed to expose their bodies to the view of men and were not supposed to have sex or become pregnant during this period. But they associated and interacted among themselves. Among the things they learned were hair styling, body painting and decorating, singing, dancing and composition of songs, most of which were love songs. They kept their skins smooth and soft by rubbing regularly a skin toning preparation called *do*.

The groom period was concluded by a big outing dance at the main town square, which attracted crowds of spectators from all parts of the district. For the first time after many years, the girls exposed their well-cult'red and decorated bodies in a great cultural dance of maidens, with great cheering by crowds of admirers, well-wishers, parents, friends and relatives. Gifts and presents were made to them. Before this time, some prospective husbands had already ear-marked the girls they would marry.

Thus within days and weeks after this great dance of maidens at the town square, all the girls got married.

After marriage and after the birth of their first child, each husband arranged for his wife to perform the feminine *Yaa*, which consisted of simple rituals and ceremonies, the cost being borne by the husbands. The ceremony took place at the compound of the wife's parents and lasted for about a week or two, and was witnessed by close relatives, friends, and well-wishers.

With that ceremony, the young woman was said to have gained excellence in spirit life, and could be as wise and as intelligent in the spirit world as her husband. And if her husband was rich enough to perform an outing called Bogo for her, she became a member of the upper social class and could move with and interact freely among women of that class without restrictions. As a matter of fact, it was the men who had performed the *Yaagẽ* tradition who also performed the feminine *Yaa* traditional rite and the Bogo outing for their wives. In that way, they were able to elevate their wives to the same social status and to the same level of spiritual intelligence as themselves.

Chapter Six

Impact on Modern Youth Organisations in the Niger Delta

1. General Overview

The movement for the Survival of Ogoni People (MOSOP) is a well-known modern youth organization in the Niger Delta of Nigeria, with a focus on Ogoniland. It derived its organizational principles from the *yaa* tradition of Ogoni. Unfortunately, only the MOSOP elders understood the ideology and discipline of the *yaa* tradition. The vast majority of the youths who formed the vanguard of MOSOP, called National Youth Council of Ogoni People (NYCOP) did not know anything concerning the ideology of the *yaagẽ* tradition. As a result they committed serious offences. At the organisational level, MOSOP was like the *yaa* tradition because of its grassroots basis. Likewise at the personal level, the relationship between the NYCOP youths and the MOSOP elders was similar to that between the *yaa* men and the *yaa* fathers (*tẹ-yaa*). Thus the *yaa* father was like a great father and the *yaa* men were his great sons who, by virtue of their training, understood and lived the rules of success in life.

Although a similar relationship existed between the NYCOP youths and the MOSOP elders, the relationship was traditionally lacking in depth. The youth's knowledge of the traditional ideology was extremely shallow or non-existent. In the traditional setting, the individual *yaa* man was trained for character, integrity and with a high sense of the sanctity of the human life, to the extent that there were taboos and strict sanctions safe-guarding it. For example, although it was lawful for the *yaa* men to carry their weapons publicly as an insignia of their social status, yet it was a taboo for any body to wound or harm another person with a weapon or an object such that blood dropped on the ground. Whenever such happened (which was rare), a heavy fine of money, including a goat for ritual cleansing of the land, was traditionally invoked.[45] This traditional law or taboo was active throughout every Ogoni village. Nonetheless, nowadays it has been seriously undermined by the police and the modern court system which, more often than not, lets the culprits go free. Assassinations, murder or killing of people on Ogoni soil was unheard of, as the traditional punishment was very severe. The MOSOP youths lacked this traditional ideological awareness. As a result several cases of murder were reported against them, which became the cause of a rift between them and the elders.

Secondly, the relationship between the NYCOP youths and the MOSOP elders was also lacking in content. Whereas the individual *yaa* man was trained to be diligent, hardworking and self-reliant in the traditional occupations for life under the close supervision of a house father (*te-be*), the NYCOP youths of MOSOP had no such privilege and no such training. In fact, many of the NYCOP youths were unemployed able-bodied youths, who were looking for avenues to vent their youthful energies but lacking the traditional discipline and responsibility. Unlike the *yaa* men, whose training focused on responsibility and future leadership, many of the NYCOP youths were not really sure if there was a hopeful future for them. Hence their level of self-discipline was low.

The result of this lack of traditional depth and discipline was the Giokoo tragedy, which occurred on 21st May, 1994. Ten years before that, in March 1984, I had had the rare privilege of a personal interview with the late King of Gokana, His Majesty J.P. Bagia, who told me everything about the place called Giokoo, and about the early history of Gokana. Now talking about traditional taboos and laws, Giokoo is a clear example of a centre of traditional taboos in Ogoniland, which means that it was a restricted place. Historically, it was a meeting place for comrade warriors, having a common vision, common goal, and common objectives, to consider issues of national significance. For that reason, strong traditional mechanisms to punish deviancy, treachery, and subversion against a citizen or the fatherland, were in place there. It was therefore a big safety damaging mistake for the MOSOP elders to have met in that place to discuss highly sensitive political questions in which there were bitter disagreements against fellow citizens (traditional taboos violated). The traditional mechanisms placed there by the founding fathers re-acted swiftly. The result was what has now become known in our history as the "Giokoo tragedy", in which four top Ogoni political chieftains were killed. The tragedy caused the final wreck of the glorious MOSOP yacht. But the remote cause or the build up to it was the deficiency in the traditional discipline and training of the NYCOP youths. This was a serious contrast to the sound discipline and the all-round training of the *yaa* men of the *yaagẽ* tradition.

From the foregoing analysis, we may go further to cite more areas of contrast between the *yaagẽ* tradition and the modern youth organisations in Ogoniland. Again with MOSOP as our case study, we can cite the areas of strength in the *yaagẽ* tradition, as against weaknesses in the MOSOP organisation, and by extension in other modern youth organizations in the Niger Delta.

2. Proper Supervision of the Youths

In the *Yaagẽ* tradition, there was strict supervision of the youths at several levels. At the top, the *tẹ yaa* (*yaa* father) was strictly supervised by the council of elders; his character, integrity, and moral rectitude from youth, were scrutinized and approved before he was allowed to start the *Yaawĩi* tradition, under which the youths performed the *yaagẽ* tradition. At the level of the youths, each youth or *yaa* man was under close supervision and training by two men known as house fathers (*tẹ be*), who were selected and appointed by the youth's parents on the basis of their character and integrity. The parents also continued to monitor their performance throughout the duration of the traditional exercise. Because of this, the house fathers put in their best efforts to make sure that they produced a man of honour for the society; and that, out of sheer patriotism without monetary reward.

At the palm wine camp (*nuloo*), where most of the training took place, each youth's character and integrity was rigorously tested in several subtle ways. Such character traits as tendency to stealing, lying, truancy, deviancy, dishonesty, etc. were carefully noted, unknown to the individual youths. For example at the *nuloo* (palm wine camp), one of the most important ways of detecting character was through eating. The popular food eaten at the *nuloo* was the elder's favourite dish, yam foofoo, which was served very hot. The food was not shared. Everybody, both the elders and the youths ate in one large wooden bowl or trough. The whole yam foofoo was put in it and a pot of hot boiling soup was emptied on top of it together with all the fish or bush meat. Eating started immediately.

The shy or slow youths usually ended up starving, because there was no reserve food. The 'smart' youth would eat but how would he eat? Would he go for the meat or for the food first? Which piece of meat or lump of fish would he take? Suppose his favourite piece of meat or fish was on the other side of the bowl, should he cross his hand over the food to take it? Or should he shift the bowl? Or should he just leave it? Suppose the food was not going to be enough to his satisfaction, should he scoop some in his palm, since it was likely that others would eat more than he?

What about other people's hands in the bowl? Should he be mindful not to wet other people's hands with soup? Should he just go ahead and eat as much as he could, since if he didn't, others might eat more than he? What about the elder eating next to him? Should he wait for the elder to remove his hand from the bowl before he puts his own, or should he just go ahead and put in his hand along side the elder's hand because if he did not do so, he might end up eating less food while others eat more? What about his hands. Should he wash his hands? Suppose by doing so he misses a favourite sitting position? Alternatively, should he wash his hands in good time before the food was ready, so that when the food was ready, he would just sit down and begin to eat? Or should he continue to do his work until he hears the announcement that food is ready? What about the youth who sees a game struggling in somebody else's snare, should he take it, if only to prevent it from escaping? Or should he report it at the *nuloo*? What about fish in somebody else's fish trap in the water? Should the youth take it? Or should he report it?

No one knows the answers to these questions. As a matter of fact, this writer had eaten with the elders at the palm wine camp (*nuloo*) and had gone through these experiences without knowing the true nature of the goings on until much later in life after listening to the conversations of the elders and hearing their remarks and comments on life.

Nonetheless, I could tell that I performed well from the openness of the elders to me and from their good wishes, such as "well done", "you are our hope". A concrete example was in 1968, during the heat of the Nigerian civil war (1967–70). My uncle, His Royal Majesty M.D.K. Tornwe II, the Gbenemene I of Babbe Kingdom, had abdicated. Without prior information, the elders invited me into his presence in the palace and asked me to stand in their midst. Then they put a bottle of gin into the hand of my uncle and asked him to pass it round me and say in libation that he had handed the rulership to me. My uncle did it without argument. I was surprised. I went back to my father's house and consulted with my elder brother, as our own father had died nine years back in 1960. I told my brother that I was already a consecrated minister of God, and that I was not keen on combining the two offices. My brother agreed with me. So I went back to the palace where the elders were still gathered. I thanked them for their great love for me by bestowing on me the rulership of the town in the position of my uncle. I expressed my appreciation to them. But I also told them that something was bothering me. When I was consecrated as a minister of God, I took an oath that I would serve God faithfully; that if I accepted the position and function of a chief in addition, it would contradict the oath which I took. They saw with me immediately; and without argument they released me from accepting the office.

Although few months after that, my uncle was arrested by the Nigerian Army and detained at the Kirikiri Prison in Lagos for over three years, the elders did not appoint any one else to the position, not even any of my uncle's sons or relations. The position remained vacant until my uncle was finally released in 1971, and brought home. He resumed his rulership of Boue Kingdom as well as the Gbenemene I of Babbe, a position he maintained until his death in June 1975.

I have cited this incident to prove that as a youth, I passed through the various levels of youth experience and was supervised and observed by the elders and found approved for leadership. I know that many men and women of my age who are alive today also passed through similar experiences and were found approved for leadership by the elders of their communities.

What is the degree of supervision and character observation in the modern youth organisations in Ogoniland today? Again consider the case of the National Youth Council of Ogoni People (NYCOP), which is the vanguard of MOSOP. What do we know about the character of its leaders? How much supervision was there among the NYCOP youths, which had branches in almost every Ogoni village? Our study shows that there was little or no supervision on their day-to-day activities. They took unilateral decisions at the local level and took actions, which even the elders would hesitate to contemplate. For example, those youths executed a chief in Nyokana in 1993, whom they accused of practising witchcraft against the youths. At Nokuri village in Boue Kingdom, a similar accusation was levelled against a medicine man in 1993. In that year, the medicine man was 'necklaced' and killed by the local branch of NYCOP in that village without the knowledge or authority of the NYCOP central executive, not even to talk of the MOSOP elders. These incidents terrorized the traditional rulers, so that some of them had to vacate their domains into exile in Port Harcourt.

This matter was the subject of a MOSOP elders meeting held at Igbo Ukwu Street, D-Line, Port Harcourt, on 31st December, 1993, to which I was invited. The matter of the indiscipline and lawlessness of the NYCOP youths was the only item on the agenda. All the key elders were present, except the new president of MOSOP, Mr Ken Saro-Wiwa. The former president, Dr. G. B. Leton, was presiding. Other elders present were Chief E. N. Kobani, Chief S. N. Orage, Chief E. A. Apenu, Chief T. N. Nwieke, Mr. T. B. Rornwini, Mr. Simeon Idemyor and several others whose names I cannot now recall. The whole house condemned the actions of the youths but the majority blamed it on Saro-Wiwa, because, as they pointed out, it was he alone who had ultimate control over the NYCOP youths. In the heat of the debate a motion was introduced that Saro-Wiwa should be arrested and detained, and that a letter should be written to the then Military Government requesting troops to be stationed in Ogoniland, which would protect the people against the militant NYCOP youths. When it seemed that the motion was becoming almost unanimous, because nobody spoke against it, I stood up to oppose the motion. I told the elders that in my position as a historian and as a man of God, I could foresee the danger in the proposed action. I told the house that what was happening in Ogoniland was a revolution; that in history, a revolution is caused by a "spirit force", which rests on a single individual; that in the case of Ogoni, that individual was Ken Saro-Wiwa; that in a traditional setting, based on my study of Ogoni tradition, what the elders used to do, was to find out the individual on whom this "spirit force" rests. Once that individual had been identified, all the elders used to rally round that individual to give him their support, while at the same time sinking their personal differences or disagreements. I appealed to them to do the same with Saro-Wiwa; that if they did so, all what they set out to achieve would be achieved. While I was still speaking, I could notice several of the elders shuffling their feet on the floor in disapproval. Nonetheless, after the speech, it seemed that the motion was dropped, as no one else spoke again on it. The meeting ended; and food and drinks were served. Whether the matter was dropped indefinitely for good, or simply shelved for another day, this is now history. But one thing I am sure of is that, if my advice had been heeded by the elders, the Giokoo tragedy would have been avoided.

3. Relationship Between the Youths and the Elders

What is the relationship between the youths of the modern organizations and the elders in the various communities? In many communities in the Niger Delta, including Ogoni, the youths are at variance with the elders. They arm themselves or are armed by persons, other than the community elders, for selfish purposes. They receive bribes from the oil companies in the name of the communities, bypassing the elders, who are the accredited leaders of the communities. On the other hand, the elders of some communities receive gratifications from the oil companies for their personal enrichment without using such money to develop the communities or for the benefit of the youths. In such a situation, the communities become the loser, as the oil companies exploit this state of affairs to cheat the communities. Where the elders are truly men of integrity, the truism in the saying remains, which states "what an elder can see sitting down, a youth cannot see standing up". Whatever the case, these young persons are not wise and experienced enough to take diplomatic decisions or actions on behalf of communities.

In the *yaagẽ* tradition, the relationship between the youths and the elders was intimate and strong and lasted for life. It meant that, apart from his own blood father and mother, the youth became the son of as many fathers (elders) as possible and the elder became the father of as many sons as possible. In fact, that was the actual meaning of the word *Yaawĩi* (rite of sons). At the personal level, the relationship between the *tẹ be* (house father) and the *dam yaa* (*yaa* man or youth) was very intimate and life-long. In age, the *tẹ be* or house father was a bridge between the youth and the youth's blood father. In every significant progress in the youth's life, such as when he wanted to erect an attachment to his father's house, in order to have his own separate room, the *tẹ be* was formally informed with a jar of palm wine. The youth and the *tẹ be* together carried this jar of palm wine to meet with the father of the youth to discuss the idea. And when the actual work was carried out, the *tẹ be* was there on the spot to supervise and direct the work according to the directive of the youth's father.

Annually, on the occasion of the feast of *Yọwĩdam* (feast of war or of manhood or manly male), the youth carried a special present to his house father (*tẹ be*). This was a log of smouldering wood and a jar of palm wine. Smouldering wood was used as heating fuel for the homes of the elderly. This present was very important to the elders, who needed to keep warm always, especially at nights. it is to be noted that in those days when there was no electricity, no kerosene, no matches; smouldering wood was greatly needed, especially by the elders. whose homes were colder than the women houses, where a lot of cooking was done, which kept the women's houses warmer at nights than the men's houses. So we can see in this example, a very significant caring relationship that existed between the youths of the *Yaagé* tradition and their elders throughout life. Now take a look inside our colleges and universities, how many of our undergraduates remember their supervisors, who supervised their long essays to enable them to graduate and obtain their first degrees or first titles in life? How many masters and doctoral students remember the professors and senior lecturers, who tortuously supervised their theses and dissertations? In the villages, how many of the politicians, ministers, senators, commissioners, ambassadors, businessmen, etc. who are now in Abuja, Lagos, Port Harcourt, overseas, etc., remember the poor villages left behind and the poor conditions in the villages, where they grew up? The poor villagers still scoop their drinking water from the old surface streams. The old village school (if they had one) either remains the same or is badly dilapidated and without sitting facilities. The children are more illiterate now than when he or she was a child there some forty or fifty years ago. Yet these are the Nigerians who wallow in millions and billions of dollars stuck away in overseas banks, and meanwhile here in Nigeria, they live in luxurious mansions in Lagos, Abuja, and Port Harcourt, etc. from where they continue to grab or divert the little crumbs that would trickle down to the rural communities through their network of political and contracting associations.

4. Talents by Character Identification Among the Youths

I have referred to the observation of character among the youths through group eating or dinners at the palm wine camp (*nuloo*). Observation of character was also done on many other areas of life during the *Yaagẽ* traditional training, such as during group activity or communal work. How did each youth perform during such activities? Which youths had the capacity to initiate new ideas or new approach to the particular task or problem? Did some youths have the capacity to perform better working alone or working in small groups? Which youths have begun to introduce some new ideas into their village or communities, such as organizing the cleaning of the town square, the access road to the village stream, or erecting an enclosure for changing clothes after bathing in the village public stream? Which youths have introduced some social clubs in which they try to practise some of the arts in imitation of the elders? These were some of the areas in which the elders observed character types, ability, creativity and talent among the youths. This enabled the elders to note the youths endowed with true leadership qualities and began to provide subtle guidance and acceptability.

Is such observation of youth talent and character available today? Of course, our pre-civil war educational system had a measure of these observations of youths character but since the civil war (1967-70) and since the era of the military, these values have disappeared from our educational system. In the case of the NYCOP youths, what did the MOSOP elders know about the character of the NYCOP youths, from their leaders down to their followership? Was there any ideology or code of conduct guiding the NYCOP youths? Was there a system of leadership measurement applicable to the NYCOP youths? The answer to all these questions is, "None".

Consider the society itself. What kind of youths do our political chieftains gather around themselves. Why is the nomenclature 'thugs' applied to them? Yet these are supposed to be the leaders of tomorrow. If the youths of today are taught and armed to kill their fellow citizens, what will happen when these youths become leaders tomorrow? Public office holders who are today's elders, cheat and steal large amounts of public funds and distort public service; and the youths know it! What guts have such leaders or public officers to tell the youths that to do so is a crime? The youths may tolerate them because of their relative weakness but they do not respect or honour them from their hearts.

What about the character of our youths in the colleges and universities today? Consider the cases of widespread examination malpractices and impersonations at public examinations etc. Consider the cases of corruption by public examinations invigilators. What legacies are the elders of today leaving for our youths, who are to be leaders tomorrow? The candidate who passes an examination knows that he has passed because he has been aided to cheat, and the one who fails knows that he or she would probably have passed had not the so-called invigilators aided some candidates to cheat. The unemployed university graduate roaming the streets, knows that he is jobless because some officers, directors, or elders at the head of a government department, company or parastatal, had blocked him and sold his job to the highest bidder or kinsman, or stolen the money that would have expanded the industry to enable it to absorb him.

Is there any wonder then that in the universities and colleges, the modern youth has gone underground, only to re-emerge as cultists, in which guise they now carry out what their elders are doing in society. Consider this phenomenon called 'ghost workers' commonly found in the civil service and in government owned companies and parastatals? Whose creation is it?

Nigerian elders boast of "waging war" against corruption. What is corruption? You cannot fight an enemy you do not know. Corruption is a spirit. Flesh and blood cannot fight a spirit. In the Christian Bible, it is called covetousness or greed. This is the spirit Jesus strictly warned Christians against. Unfortunately for Nigeria, this spirit has also invaded the Christian churches and has turned many of the so-called Christian warriors over as its willing 'recruits', 'allies' and 'agents'. Nigerians must wake up to the reality of the danger of this destructive spirit, which has eaten deep into the very roots of our society.

5. Character Within the Elders' Cadre

In the traditional society, the elders were united at every point in time. The elders were men who had passed through the crucibles of life. They understood the needs of society. Accordingly, they were dedicated to providing such needs. In fact the pre-occupation of solving and providing social needs constituted the very blood and sinus of their being. That was why not every one could be an elder. Mere possession of money could not make one an elder. The primary qualification for an elder was character, intelligence, integrity and ability. If a youth possessed these qualities, the elders could assist him to have money as well. I suppose that was what Chinua Achebe meant in *Things Fall Apart*[47], when he talked about a youth called Okonkwo! In the traditional setting, an elder was a leader of no mean character.

Taking their queue from the traditional examples at the inception of MOSOP, the elders were well-united. Like the traditional elders, they all understood the problems the Ogoni were facing; and they were all vigorously seeking ways and means to solve those problems. Among these problems were the denial of qualitative education to Ogoni children , denial of job opportunities to Ogoni indigenes, the stark poverty in Ogoniland, and non-consideration of Ogoni sons and daughters for governmental appointments at Federal and State levels. Others were Shell's exploitation of Ogoni environment and natural resources and its denial of Ogoni indigenes of jobs, contracts, training and scholarships (Appendix I).

One afternoon in 1992, Chief E. N. Kobani, myself and Mr. Ken Saro-Wiwa, were in the latter's office at 24, Aggrey Road, Port Harcourt, contemplating on these problems. Saro-Wiwa brought out an old group photograph of Ogoni traditional rulers, taken together with a British Colonial Officer in the 1930s. In that photograph, we could notice that the Ogoni traditional rulers at that time looked fresher, better nourished and better clad than the Ogoni traditional rulers in the 1990s. On the other hand, we also noticed that in the 1990s, their counterparts in the other ethnic groups in Nigeria were getting the better side of life, using money derived from Ogoni oil by Shell. The natural question then was, how long would Ogoni people continue like this? Meanwhile Ogoni children, youths and elders, were dying avoidable deaths from poverty, hunger, and disease; and the Ogoni children, who survive continue to be without the basic education and were unconsciously growing up into an adult life of poverty and deprivation for the rest of their lives!

These were the problems the founders or elders of MOSOP, under the leadership of Dr G. B. Leton, were cracking their heads to tackle. At that time, MOSOP was still a very narrow elite organization, yet to find its feet and direction. It was unknown to the generality of Ogoni people, and even to most educated Ogoni; and it did not yet have a single affiliate body. Its constitution was still being debated and fine-tuned (Appendix II).

Thus at a meeting of the elders, held on 14 September, 1992, at the residence of the president, Dr G. B. Leton, at Plot 207 Evo Road, GRA Phase II, Port Harcourt, a committee was set up to do a paper, mapping out a direction for the young movement. The following were the members of the committee:

1. Dr. N. A. Ndegwe   Chairman
2. Dr. Pius Kinako   Member
3. Dr. (Rev.) Sonpie Kpone-Tonwe Member
4. Dr. Don Baridam   Member

The committee was directed to submit its report within two weeks.

6. The Constitutional Question

The military regime of President Ibrahim Babangida was coming to an end and the political atmosphere in the country was becoming agitated. Many political pundits had predicted that the country was on the verge of disintegration. Meanwhile nominations were going on to elect a constituent assembly, which would review the 1979 constitution in preparation for federal elections and the handover of power to a a civilian government in 1993. Although some MOSOP elders had indicated their interest as candidates for nomination to the constituent assembly, the threat to the corporate existence of Nigeria was ever very ominous. What would be the fate of Ogoni people in such an eventuality? What form would such a disintegration take? Thus the committee was instructed to consider the following questions and recommend a way out for Ogoni people.

(a) Would Nigeria disintegrate in chaos?

(b) Would it be a disintegration through negotiation?

(c) Would it be a restructuring of the country through Sovereign National Conference?

(d) Would Nigeria continue to be a Federation as presently constituted?

The committee held its inaugural meeting at the country home of th Chairman at Nonwa, Tee, on 20 September 1992. At this first meeting, the committee elected this writer as its Secretary.

The most important achievement of the committee at this first meeting was to draw up a calendar of meetings, after which the chairman and his beautiful wife, treated the members to an exquisite Ogoni traditional hospitality.

The next meeting of the committee was held at the official residence of the chairman at the Rivers State University of Science and Technology (RSUST), Nkpolu, Port Harcourt. As secretary of the committee, I made sure at that meeting that I got the views of the members on each of the four points listed above. As a matter of fact, the elders listed those four points in their descending order of importance in terms of their relative criticality in the circumstances.

By the third meeting of the committee, which was scheduled for 10 October 1992, the chairman was no longer available, having received a Federal appointment as Rivers State Commissioner for the Oil Mineral Producing Areas Development Commission (OMPADEC). Consequently, attendance by the other members also dwindled. As a matter of fact, the meeting of 10 October was deemed as postponed, as no critical decision could be taken without the sanction of the chairman, and as at that moment, there was no clear explanation concerning the movement of the chairman. Information about his new appointment only filtered to us after some days. Thus, the whole work of the committee fell squarely on the shoulders of the secretary. By the calendar of the committee, at the fourth and final meeting, which was to take place on Saturday 17 October 1992, the Secretary was to present a draft report to the committee for vetting.

The facts of the abrupt absence of the chairman and the subsequent absence of the other members, which disrupted the scheduled meetings of the committee were good enough reasons for any Secretary not to submit a draft report because there would be little or nothing to report. But the matter before the committee was so crucial that no reason could be good enough not to do something about the work of the committee. So I got down to do what I could. I was happy that on the second day of meeting, the members deliberated very critically and constructively on all the four questions raised by the elders. Whatever else remained, I knew that I could 'fill in the gaps' drawing on my expert knowledge of Ogoni history, traditions and culture.

At that meting of 3rd October 1992, the members critically drew on their knowledge of history and politics and realistically reversed the elders' order of priority. Thus the committee recommended as follows:

1. That Nigeria was likely to continue to be a Federation as presently structured, either:
    (i) Under a Military Administration; or
    (ii) Under a Civilian Administration
2. That the next best option likely to occur, because of its suitability for a pluralistic polity like Nigeria, was Restructuring through a National Sovereign Conference.

The committee dropped the other two options as most unlikely to occur. In each of the two cases predicted above, Ogoni's option was to remain a part of Nigeria but should seek an autonomous status, which would enable her to have control over, at least, part of her natural resources for the development of her people, culture and environment.

Having dealt with those political questions, the rest of the report concentrated on Ogoni itself. The report stressed the point that if MOSOP was to make any impact or headway, it had to look inwards. Was there anything in Ogoni's roots and culture upon which MOSOP could draw strength to move forward? What was it that made Ogoni in pre-colonial times to live peacefully, successfully and on equal terms with her neighbours, both big and small? One of the things that came to my mind to which I drew the attention of the elders, was the principles of the *Yaa* tradition. This was very important because, if MOSOP was to become a movement to be reckoned with in Nigeria, it had to carry all Ogoni people along. It had to be the people's movement, not just of a few educated elite. It had to be a movement, which the people at the grassroots understand and belong to. MOSOP must draw on the traditional organization and the principles of the *Yaa* tradition. In short, this was summarized in the following three statements:[48]

1. A vigorous and sustained campaign spear-headed by Ogoni leaders and a supportive elite should be mounted to educate and arouse a consciousness in every Ogoni indigene - man, woman and child - about the threat to their existence as a people in Nigeria;

2. Every Ogoni indigene should be taught the practical and psychological ways of resisting humiliation and extinction, whether as individuals or as groups;

3. The focus of this campaign should be the unity of all sections of Ogoni as one indivisible ethnic nationality, despite their pursuit of political diversity in different party affiliations.

I packaged a draft report which was exactly eleven pages (type-written) and signed as Secretary, with provisions for the Chairman and other members of the committee to sign. I personally distributed the copies to all the members at their homes, some days before the final meeting scheduled for October 17, 1992, with a note that members should read the draft report and make comments: that the comments would be collated at the meeting for inclusion in the final report. I passed the Chairman's copy under his door at RSUST, because nobody was at home when I came and the door was shut.

On Saturday 17 October, I arrived at the Chairman's house at RSUST at 5 p.m., the usual time of meeting, only to find that the door was again shut. I waited for about 30 minutes, there was no sign of any person, and none of the other committee members showed up. I was angry, because I alone knew the effort I had made in the production of the report and the pressure I had put on my two daughters, Leyo and Lebeabu, who edited and typed the report in time to enable me to meet the deadline; and now it was all a wasted effort, it seemed. In that mood I returned back to Uniport. The meeting had not taken place.

I later learned that the Chairman had taken the copy I passed under his door and submitted it to the then President of MOSOP and Chairman of the elders, Dr G. B. Leton, and that the latter and the other elders had received the report with mixed feelings, except Ken Saro-Wiwa, who grabbed the report. Of the other members of the committee, who received copies, only Dr (now Professor) Don Baridam returned his copy to me later with one or two minor corrections, which informed me that he approved the draft report.

Now, why did the other elders receive the report with mixed feelings? Three explanations may be adduced. The first was political. By the terms of Article 2 section (e), sub-section (i) of MOSOP constitution, MOSOP was not to involve itself in partisan politics (Appendix II). This was where the other elders did not find in the Report matters that related to their particular interests, namely, Ogoni's nomination to the on-coming Constituent Assembly at Abuja and matters about the Federal elections in 1993.

The second was something about Ogoni's Constitutional position. Two persons among the elders were interested in the Constituent Assembly with different constitutional positions. Mr. Ken Saro-Wiwa wanted to go there to reject the 1979 constitution, because it usurped Ogoni people's rights to their land and natural resources. Dr G. B. Leton wanted to go with a more moderate approach to issues, and to toe the line of his political party. These were partisan issues, which required the consensus of a committee and the endorsement of its Chairman. In the circumstances in which the Report was written, such divisive political issues could not be deliberated upon. The Report was therefore silent on these politically divisive issues, but concentrated on the weightier issues of MOSOP and the fate of Ogoni people in Nigeria.

The third matter responsible for the cold attitude of some of the elders towards the Report, was lack of understanding of the technicalities of the Report. Prior to this time, I had done two seminars in Port Harcourt on the *Yaa* tradition; and Ken Saro-Wiwa had copies of my papers on the subject, which means that he had read and understood the *Yaa* tradition of the Ogoni. That was why he grasped the importance of the Report and grabbed it. The other elders could have gained this knowledge if the Report had been presented formally, so as to enable me to explain and defend some footnotes in the Report.

Saro-Wiwa took complete possession of the Report, carrying it daily in his brief case and constantly referring to it. He implemented the Report to the letter by touring all sections of Ogoniland, addressing the various groups - elders, traditional rulers, chiefs, men, women, youths, societies, clubs, associations etc., and recruiting them as affiliates of MOSOP. Within weeks, the popularity of Saro-Wiwa soared in Ogoniland. He completely eclipsed the other elders, including the president of MOSOP, Dr G. B. Leton.

Whatever little political differences between Dr G. B. Leton and Ken Saro-Wiwa widened and became a gulf. Thus any attempt by the other elders to regain their pre-eminence in Ogoniland only ended in pushing them deeper into the camp of the government which, inadvertently, also includes Shell, the deadly enemies of the Ogoni people. This, I suppose, was part of the background to the motion at the elders' meeting of 31st December 1993, earlier referred to above.

Meanwhile, to build up his own support base, Saro-Wiwa had gone ahead to recruit new members into the leadership of MOSOP, persons, who did not know the pains, the compassion, the self-less motive and the head-cracking experience, which the original elders or founders of MOSOP went through before they founded the organization and brought it to limelight. (Appendix I). They merely came on board more or less like pleasure cruisers! To them it did not matter what happened to the boat, the Ogoni people, so long as they could continue to enjoy the cruise. With the support of this new breed of leadership, Saro-Wiwa finally became the President of MOSOP, and with that, he convinced the masses of Ogoni people to boycott the voting in the 1993 Federal elections, as a protest against the ills of the 1979 Constitution against Ogoni people.

In conclusion, the foregoing analysis represents the inside mechanisms and motions within the circle of the elders, which finally made MOSOP to become what it became and what it ceased to become. Are there any lessons, which other modern youth organizations in the Niger Delta and, indeed, Nigeria, can learn from the experiences of MOSOP?

Chapter Seven

Conclusion

MOSOP's success in social mobilization and grassroots organization stimulated the formation of many youth organisations not only in the Niger Delta but also in the wider Nigeria during the period from about the mid-1990s through 2000 and 2001. In the Niger Delta, the most notable among these nascent organisations was the Ijọ Peoples Council (IPC) Outside the Niger Delta, Oodua Peoples Congress (OPC) emerged among the Yoruba of south-western Nigeria. The Arewa Peoples Congress (APC) also sprang up among the Hausa/Fulani of Northern Nigeria, followed by the Bakassi Boys, which flourished among the Igbo of South Eastern Nigeria. Apart from these, there were also parallel elders' organisations, such as *Afenifere* among the Yoruba, Ijọ National Congress (INC) among the Ijọ, *Ohaneze*, among the Igbo, and 'Arewa Consultative Forum' (ACF) among the Hausa/Fulani. But only few of these organisations could trace back their history beyond a few years. Groups like OPC and *Ohaneze* actually came into being in 2000 AD to provide a response to the frequent killings of Southerners in Northern Nigeria by Muslim youths within months after the hand-over of power by the military in May, 1999.[49] As for the Bakassi Boys, this group also came into being in 2000 AD, possibly in the same circumstance as *Ohaneze* and OPC but they eventually gained the patronage of the Governments of Abia and Anambra States, against armed robbers. But their self-discipline and brand of justice have been a matter of serious concern both nationally and internationally.[50]

Unlike the youths of the *Yaa* tradition, the youths of these modern organisations had no historical tradition, no ideological foundation, and no philosophical direction. They existed only as appendages of the contemporary political establishments and were manipulated by the political machine in each state or region and, in some cases, by the religious superstructure. They were therefore, prone to acts of extreme lawlessness, piracy, violence, and murder because they lacked the stabilization of firm historical roots, or the guidance of a clear traditional or national ideology. As a result some of them fell under the wrath of the Federal Government. The cases of Odi massacre (2000 AD), Tiv massacre (2002 AD), Tiv/Jukun killings, Kano, Kaduna religious killings, Jos religious killings, Lagos killings, Zaakpon and Yeghe killings (2002 AD) etc., are historical examples.[51] Youth organizations which engage in such acts cannot be said to hold the future of any nation, since a house divided against itself cannot stand (Jesus).[52] Similarly, a nation divided against itself cannot stand. It is evident therefore, that youths of this breed hold no future for anybody, not even for themselves.

It is obvious, therefore, that this country cannot continue in this way, as its youths are being regularly and systematically destroyed both directly and indirectly. Something has to be done quickly. The country's youths are in dire need of strong philosophical and psychological re-orientation.

There is need for a well-defined ideological direction. The youths must be made to know early enough that they have a future to live for and a national ideology or doctrine to defend. They must know that they owe a sacred duty to God, to themselves and to fatherland, to protect and defend every citizen of this country anywhere and at any time. There must be a strong ideology which will make the killing or maiming of a citizen or any person on the soil of this country a culpable taboo throughout the country. Such a taboo should have pre-eminence over all religious or sectional sentiments. In the present circumstances, this is a daunting task. But the solution will not come from Europe or America. No philosopher or genius outside this country can solve this problem for our country. The solution must come from the citizens, the culture and the soil of this country. That is why we make bold to point out that the *Yaa* tradition has something excellent to offer for our youths or for leadership training in this country. With its principles and discipline at our disposal, what will be required are the integrity, sincerity, commitment and devotion of the patrons and leaders, whose honour it will be to implement and practicalize them.

The *Yaa* tradition as a philosophy, has all the potentials necessary to turn the youths of this country around for a better future. Its ideological foundation is excellent for leadership training; its discipline is a formidable antidote against indolence, indiscipline, cultism, truancy, drug-abuse, immodesty, asexuality or sexual perversion, corruption, rapacity, profanity, desecration and ungodliness. Youth leaders and patrons need to study the principles of the *Yaa* tradition with a view to applying them to today's youths and youth organisations. Youth leaders and patrons ought to redress themselves with a thorough knowledge of the *Yaa* tradition, in order to imbibe and inculcate the rudiments of cultured or quality leadership, or leadership for a higher tomorrow, and vow to cultivate such quality leadership in the youths being committed to them.

Unfortunately, this type of quality youth leadership has been lacking in this country since the days of the military dictatorship. What we have been seeing in this country is a situation where a politician uses his position as a leader to gather a group of youths around himself, gives them a name, money (public funds), and equipment, and sends them out to 'protect' his interest against the interest of a rival politician and, or against the interest of the very society the politician was elected to represent! Such youths are usually without the basic training in the culture and traditions of the society. Some of them do not even have the minimum educational qualifications; and those of them who have such qualifications, are without jobs. Obviously, such youths, who are without any background training and without a focus in life, can only be raised for bloodshed and self destruction. Meanwhile the university graduates are wasting away without gainful employment. A nation full of such youths is a nation without an ideology, without direction and without a future. Under such conditions, corruption and corrupting leadership are institutionalized and reproduced in cyclical evolutions. As Jesus said, a corrupt tree can only bear corrupt fruits (New Testament).[52]

In these circumstances, there is no gainsaying the fact that the principles of the *Yaa* tradition are a brightening hope for the future of our youths. As earlier stated, the *Yaa* tradition is a rich cultural material; and it is suitable for a variety of literary documentation for adoption into the national educational system. It is interesting, educative, progressive, creative, dramatic, historical, indigenous, unique, exuberant and colourful. Its principles and discipline are excellent for character formation and self-discipline. Its work ethic is ideal for inculcating a positive attitude to life by inducing a desire for hardwork, diligence, creativity and excellence. It's social code is a bastion for personal holiness, love for one another, friendship, fellowship, comradeship, respect for the elders, for human life and for that which is holy or ancient. Is not this what is needed in order to make the youths of this great country go forward for a better tomorrow? I recommend it whole-heartedly to the nation; to the leaders, to the politicians, to the workers, to every individual and to the youths themselves.

In realisation of this objective, the *Yaa* tradition should be made a course of study in our Universities, Colleges of Education, Colleges of Arts and Science, and Polytechnics. The course should be taught in Departments of Culture, History, Creative Arts, Anthropology, and Sociology. In polytechnics it should be taught in Departments/Institutes of Foundation Studies. The title of the course should be "*Yaa Tradition Culture of Ogoni*", with course code YTC 100.1 and YTC 100.2. In Universities and Colleges, it should be a two semester course at 2 credits per week per semester. The first semester should consist of lectures based on the relevant sections of this book, in addition to other supplementary material, followed with written examinations.

The second semester should consist of field trip to Ogoniland, where the students would have the opportunity to meet the traditional experts, ask questions derived from their lectures, and receive explanations, demonstrations, and further teaching. The centre of the field trip should be based at the Polytechnic, Bori, where the traditional experts from the villages would be invited to interact with the students. From there the students and their teachers or lecturers would decide to visit places of interest in the villages, in order to have a feel of the environment and perhaps, some aspects of the *nu oo* experience. Each class should make at least one of such field trips during the second semester, at the end of which there should be a written examination and report both of which should be scored. In the secondary schools, the course should be taught as part of the history of the Niger Delta.

For the purpose of moral re-orientation and self-discipline of our youths, the course should be a Faculty Course and made compulsory for all Year I students. On the creative aspect, experts from the Departments of Culture, History and Theatre Arts should come together to produce a major play called "*Dam Yaa*" or "*The Yaa Man*", in which the qualities of true leadership as enunciated in this book would be demonstrated as a mirror for the youths of this country and, indeed, the world to emulate.[53] Fortunately, for the University of Port Harcourt, there is a Department of Religion and Cultural Studies, a Department of History and Diplomatic Studies, and a Department of Creative Arts, where the noble ideas suggested in this book should begin to be put into practice. God bless Nigeria and bless Ogoniland.

References

1. Williamson, Kay, 1988. "Linguistic Evidence of the Pre-History of the Niger Delta" in E.J. Alagoa, E. N. Anozie and N. Nzewunwa (eds.), *The Early History of the Niger Delta*. Hamburg: Helmut Buske. pp. 68-119.

2. Kpone-Tonwe, Sonpie, 1990. "The Ogoni of the Eastern Niger Delta Mainland: an Economic and Political History from the Earliest Times to about 1900. Ph.D. Dissertation, University of Port Harcourt.

3. Wiliiamson, Kay, op. cit.

4. Herodotus. 1862. *History* III, Book IV, V and VI, trans. George Rawlinson London: John Murray.

5. Kpone-Tonwe, Sonpie, 1990. op. cit. p. 69 1987. "The Historical Traditions of Ogoni" Vol. II. M.Phil. Thesis University of London p. 258.

6. Pereira, Pacheco (Duarte). 1937. *Esmeraldo de situ orbis*. ed. G.H.T. Kimble. London: Hakluyt Society. 1956: *Esmeraldo de situ orbis* (vers 1506-08), trans Raymond Mauny. Bissau.

7. Barbot, James. 1732. "An abstract of a voyage to New Calabar or Rio Real in the year 1699" in A. Churchill and I, Churchill (eds.) *A Collection of Voyages and Travels*. Vol. V. London: Thomas Osborn and Henry Lintot pp. 455 - 466.

8. Kpone-Tonwe, Sonpie. 1996. "Impact of Linguistics and Oral tradition on the origin and identity of some Niger Delta place-names: Case study of the Ogoni region 1." *Nigerian Heritage: Journal of the National Commission for Museums and Monuments.* Vol. 5, pp. 100-114.

9. Rodney, Walterr, 1967. "A Reconsideration of the Mane invasions of Sierra Leone". *Journal of African History, Vol.* VIII No. 2., pp. 219-246.

10. Kpone-Tonwe, Sonpie. 2000. "Politics of the *Gbene* Title in Pre-colonial Ogoni" *Kiabara: Journal of Humanities "* (Port Harcourt). *Vol. 6 No. 2, pp. 63 - 76.*

11. Saro-Wiwa, Ken. 1991. Personal communication

12. Saro-Wiwa, Ken. 1994 One result of his sudden arrest death, and the looting of his office by soldiers, was the loss of my manuscripts, including one titled "*A History of Ogoni: An Economic and Political Analysis from Initial Settlement to 1948"* which he was to publish. Apart from the devastating effects of his execution, the loss of the manuscript was also a serious set back to my own academic progress.

13. Kpone-Tonwe, Sonpie. 1997. "Property Reckoning and Methods of accumulating wealth among the Ogoni of the eastern Niger Delta". *Africa:* Journal of International African Institute Vol. 67, No. 1, pp. 130 - 158.

14. Kpone-Tonwe, Sonpie. ibid. p. 135

15. Kpone-Tonwe, Sonpie. 1990. op. cit. p. 125.

16. Gibbons, E. J. 1932 "Intelligence Report on Ogoni" Opobo Division, Calabar Province, NAE file 28032 CSO 26/3.

17. Forde, Daryll. 1964. *Yako Studies*. International African Institute, London, Oxford University Press. p. 89.

18. Kpone-Tonwe, Sonpie. 1998. "Transportation and Economic Development in Pre-Colonial Ogoni". *The Ethnographer: Journal of Niger Delta Research Association.* Vol.1, No. 2. pp. 23 - 35.

19. In the Niger Delta, this practice is still current among some ethnic groups, e.g. among the Nembe of Ijọ and the Choba of Ikwerre.

20. Forde, Daryll, op. cit. p. 86.

21. Fortes, Mayer, 1950. "Kinship and Marriage among the Ashanti" in *African Systems of Kinship and Marriage, A. R.* Raddiffe-Brown and Daryll Forde (eds.), International African Institute (London: Oxford University Press). pp. 252 - 284.

22. Richards, Audrey I. 1950. "Some types of family structure among the central Bantu" in *African Systems of Kinship and Marriage* A. R. Raddiffe-Brown and Daryll Forde (eds.), International African Institute (London: Oxford University Press), pp. 207 - 251.

23. Kpone-Tonwe, Sonpie. 1990. op. cit. p. 27.

24. Kpone-Tonwe, Sonpie. ibid p. 251.

25. Kpone-Tonwe, Sonpie. ibid p. 248

26. Kpone-Tonwe, Sonpie. 2001 "Leadership Training in Pre-colonial Nigeria: The *Yaa* tradition of Ogoni" *International Journal of African Historical Studies.* Vol. 34, No. 2 (2001). 385-403.

27. Zim: was the name given to the spirits of those ancestors who obtained the highest title of *Gbene* and became possessing spirits. For details about ancestral spirits in Ogoni, their social and politics activities, see Kpone-Tonwe, Sonpie. "Politics of the *Gbene* title in Pre-colonial Ogoni" *Kiabara: Journal of Humanities.* Vol. 6, No. 2, 2000, pp. 63 - 76.

28. The *te-yaa*'s pilgrimage to the matrilineage house did not imply that he had any political, economic, or inheritance link with the matrilineage. From the fifteenth or sixteenth century, this pilgrimage had become purely religious. In fact, by performing the *yaawii* tradition, the *te-yaa* was already in the process of establishing his own autonomous house.

29. *Taa eeri* means three traditional Ogoni weeks. A traditional Ogoni week is five days.

30. "*Ega*". This was the name given by the spirit medium of Gbeneyaaloo, the leader of the founding ancestors, to the weapon they carried when they landed in Nama at the initial settlement. The spirit-medium was interviewed during possession in the ancient town of Gure on 12th March 1984. S/No. 61, Tape No. Og/SK/17. Nwinedam Michael (aged 35) was the interpreter of the spirit medium, who spoke an archaic language. The interpreter was supernaturally endowed to understand.

31. Kpone-Tonwe, Sonpie, 2001. op. cit.

32. By scattering cash gifts into the crowds, the *te-yaa* was not proving that he was rich. Rather it was a traditional way of demonstrating divine generosity who scatters his goodness in nature on every body, both good and bad. The *yaa* tradition was an occasion for the successful rich man to demonstration that generosity.

33. The number seven (7) is sacred in Ogoni religion or Ogoni divinity. The phrase *ereba sõ ereba* (seven times seven) is often spoken by priests and spirits mediums during ritual incantations. Its substitute or equivalent is four (4) numbers. In a ritual action where seven numbers of an item was required, if four (4) numbers were found the ritual action would proceed. We wish to observe that there is obviously no connection or element of feedback between the ritual use of the number seven (7) in Ogoni religion and the biblical use, such as the biblical *seventy times seven* (Matt 18: 21 - 22), or the four corners and four winds of the earth (Rev. 7:11) or the seventy elders (Num 11:16), or the *seven times* dipping in the river Jordan by the leprous Naaman in order to be healed. This is because there was no knowledge of the Bible in Ogoniland until the 1930s, but long before then the mystical or ritual use of the number seven (7) had been in practice in Ogoniland. In fact, the mystical title of King Gbenesaakoo, the founder of the Kingdom of Gokana was said to be "Ereba Mene Ereba Giã" meaning "Seven Great, Seven Brave" or simply, "Seven Sevens". See Kpone-Tonwe, Sonpie, "Settlement of Ogoni on the Niger Delta Mainland". A Public Lecture to the Kagote Conference held at Suanu Finimale Nwika Hall, Bori, on 27 December 1992.

34. The significance of the fly in this context is unknown. Some informants said that it was because the fly was a dirty and unholy creature. Others thought that it was a way of ensuring that the ritual was completed before daybreak, as flies do not move about in the dark. Perhaps the original significance is still elusive.

35. Virginity was regarded as a state of purity, holiness, or innocence, and nudity without shame was a way of demonstrating that purity, holiness and innocence.

36. Kpone-Tonwe, Sonpie. 1987. op. cit. p. 111

37. Kpone-Tonwe, Sonpie. ibid p. 201

38. This holy sop, administered by the young priestess of his father's house, was supposed to give him strength throughout the race. In ancient times, this last sop was said to give the warrior enduring strength in battle, and if he did not return alive, to give him strength in the spirit world.

39. *Pa yaa* was an abstract expression representing negative spirit forces attracted to the individual participants during the performance. At the end of the performance, those negative spirit forces were sent away and banned to the sea by special simple rituals. Without that they would remain or cling to the individuals and produce negative or abnormal psychological behaviour in the individual (See Kpone-Tonwe, 1987: 203).

40. Kpone-Tonwe, Sonpie, 1987. op. cit p. 254.

41. Kpone-Tonwe, Sonpie. 1998. op. cit. pp. 23 - 35

42. Baikie, W. B. 1856. *Narrative of an Exploring Voyage up the Rivers Kwora and Binue (Commonly known as the Niger Tsadda)* in 1954. London: John Murray, (Albermarle Street). pp. 336

43. Alagoa, E. J. 1970. "Long Distance Trade and States in the Niger Delta". *Journal of African History.* Vol. 11, No. 3 pp. 319 - 329.

44. Kpone-Tonwe, Sonpie. 1996. "Impact of Linguistics and Oral Tradition on the Origin and Identity of Some Niger Delta Place Names. Case Study of the Ogoni Region 1". *Nigeria Heritage: Journal of the National Commission for Museum and Monuments.* Vol. 5, pp. 100 - 114.

45. Kpone-Tonwe, Sonpie. 1998. op. cit. p. 32.

46. Kpone-Tonwe, Sonpie. 1987. op. cit. p. 63.

47. Achebe, Chinua, 1958. *Things Fall Apart.* Greenwich, Conn.: Fawcett Publications. pp 24 - 27.

48. "The Option for Ogoni: A MCSOP Working Paper" (October 1992), p. 3.

49. *National News Leader.* April 30, 2002, p. 6

50. Amnesty International and Human Rights Watch Report. May 20, 2002.

51. *The Post Express.* Saturday May 18, 2002, pp. 1-2

52. *The New Testament of the Holy Bible*, King James Version, 1911.

53. See my earlier appeal on this subject in my article titled "Leadership Training in Pre-colonial Nigeria: The *Yaa* Traditional of Ogoni" . *The International Journal of African Historical Studies.* Vol. 34, No. 2 (2001) 85-403.

BIBLIOGRAPHY
Primary Sources
A. Oral Interviews

NAME OF INFORMANT	TAPE NO.	DAT OF INTERVIEW
AKEKUE, M. N.	---	21 Nov. 1981
	OG/SK/1,2	16 Mar. 1984
ASOO, Koobee	OG/SK/12	12 Jan. 1984
AWALA, OJI	OG/SK/21	4 Mar. 1984
BAGIA, J. P.	OG/SK/28,29	19 Feb. 1984
DEEMUA, D. D.	OG/SK/21	5 Dec. 1983
GBARATO, Adoo	OG/SK/5	18 Jan. 1984
GBEGE, Abanee	OG/SK/22	25 Nov. 1984
GININWA, G. N. K.	OG/SK/16	19 Mar. 1984
GOOKINANWAA, Ibeyo G.	OG/SK/16	19 Mar. 1984
IKPODEE, Goabere	OG/SK/19	15 Jan. 1984
IWAGBO, John	OG/SK/18	24 Mar. 1984
IWEREBE, Uranee Frank	OG/SK/19	22 Jan. 1984
KEEKEE, Dominic A.	-	24 Oct. 1981
KINANWII, Kpoko	OG/SK/11, 12	5 Jan. 1984
KPEA, Edward Nwebon	OG/SK/27	7 Feb. 1984
KPUGITA, Nnaa	OG/SK/10	2 Jan. 1984
KIRIKI, Piagbo et al.	-	17 Feb, 1990
LEGBARA, Bakoba	OG/SK/20	5 Jan. 1984
LOOLO, G. N.	OG/SK/3	25 Mar. 1984
MPEBA, Mbaedee F.	OG/SK/9	Mar. 1984
NGITO, Leelee Naabe	OG/SK/15	17 Mar. 1984
NGOFA, O. O.	OG/SK/31	4 Mar. 1984
NII, Isaanee	OG/SK/4	29 Dec. 1984
NUAKA, Lamue	OG/SK/21, 22	30 Nov. 1983 2 Dec. 1983
NWILABBA, Teetee Edamni	OG/SK/24	15 Mar. 1984

NAME OF INFORMANT	TAPE NO.	DAT OF INTERVIEW
NWINEDAM, Michael *et al.*	OG/SK/17	24 Mar. 1984
NYONE, E. B. *et al.*	OG/SK/13	26 Feb. 1984
OODEE, J. T.	OG/SK/5	30 Dec. 1983
OSARONU, J. D.	OG/SK/8	25 Feb. 1984
TEEDEE, Fredrick Buebaa	OG/SK/16	18 Mar. 1984
TIGIRI, John	OG/SK/14	10 Mar. 1984
TONWE III, A.D.	OG/SK/25, 26	21, 22 Jan. 1984

B. Published Primary Sources

Barbot, James, 1732. "An Abstract of a Voyage to New Calabar or Rio Real in the Year 1699 in Churchill and Churchill (eds.), *A Collection of Voyages and Travels*. Vol. V. (London: Thomas Osborn and Henry Lintot) pp. 455 - 466.

Baikie, W. B. 1856. *Narrative of an Exploring Voyage Up the Rivers Kwora and Binue (commonly known as the Niger Tsadda) in 1854*. London: John Murray, Albermarle Street.

Dapper, O. 1668: *Naukeurige Neschrijiving der Afrikaensche Gewestern, (Armsterdam: Jacob Van Meurs,, 2nd ed. 1676. See Het Koningrijkvan BIGUBA p. 135*.

Herodotus, 1862: *History* III, Books IV, V and VI trans. George Rawlinson. London: John Murray.

Pereira, Pacheco (Duarte) 1956: *Esmeraldo de situ Orbis* ... (Vers 1506-1508) Trans. Raymond Mauny. Bissau: Centro de Estudos de Guiné Portuguesa.

C. Archival Sources

Gibbons, E. J. 1932: "Intelligence Report on Ogoni", Opobo Division, Calabar Province. File E. P. 9595 CSE 1/85/4888.

NAE, R. P. 6378 "Proposed Ogoni Division" Opobo Division, Calabar Province.

NAE, R. P. 6402/WI. II "Ogoni Patrol Report" Ogodist, Opobo Division, Calabar Province.

Porter, J. C. 1933. "Intelligence Report on Okrika" Degema Division, Owerri Province NAE 29004 CS026/3.

Webber, H. 1931. "Intelligence Report on Bonny District". Owerri Province. NAE File 27226 CSO 26.

D. Secondary Sources:

Alagoa, E. J. 1970. "Long-distance trade and states in the Niger Delta". *Journal of African History*. Vol.II, No. 3., pp. 319 - 329.

Forde, Daryll. 1964: *Yako Studies*. International African Institute. London, Oxford University Press.

Fortes, Meyer, 1950: "Kinship and Marriage Among the Ashanti" in *African Systems of Kinship and Marriage.* A. Radcliffe-Brown and D. Forde (eds.) International African Institute. London: Oxford University Press), pp. 252 - 284.

Kpone-Tonwe, Sonpie. 1990. "The Ogoni of the Eastern Niger Delta mainland: An Economic and Political History from the earlies times to about 1900." Ph.D. dissetation, University of Port Harcourt.

Kpone-Tonwe, Sonpie. 1990. "The Historical Tradition of Ogoni". Vol II. M.Phil. Thesis. University of London.

Kpone-Tonwe, Sonpie. 1996. "Impact of liguistics and oral tradition on the origin and identity of some Niger Delta place names: A case study of the Ogoni Region I". *Nigerian Heritage: Journal of the National Commission for Museums and Monuments.* Vol 5. pp. 10C 114.

Kpone-Tonwe, Sonpie. 1997. "Property reckoning and methods of accumulating wealth among the Ogoni of the Eastern Niger Delta". *Africa: Journal of the International African Institute.* Vol 67, No. 1.

Kpone-Tonwe, Sonpie. 1998. "Transportation and Economic Development in Pre-Colonial Ogoni: Case Study of the Canoe Industry at Ko". *The Ethnographer: Journal of Niger Delta Research Association.* Vol I, No. 2, pp. 23-35.

Kpone-Tonwe, Sonpie. 2000. "Politics of the *Gbene* Title in Pre-Colonial Ogoni". *Kiabara: Journal of Humanities.* Vol 6, No. 2, pp. 63-76.

Kpone-Tonwe, Sonpie. 2001. "Leadership Training in Pre-colonial Nigeria: The Yaa Tradition of Ogoni. *International Journal of African Historical Studies.* Vol. 34, No. 2, pp. 385-403.

Kpone-Tonwe, Sonpie and Jill Salmons. 2002. "The Arts of the Ogoni". In Martha G. Anderson and Philip M. Peek (eds.) *Ways of the Rivers: Arts and Environment of the Niger Delta.* Los Angeles: UCLA Fowler Museum of Cultural History.

Rodney, Walter. 1967. "A Reconstruction of the Mane Invasions of Sierra Leone". *Journal of African History.* Vol. VIII, No. 2, pp. 219-246.

Williamsom, Kay. 1988. "Linguistic Evidence of the Pre-history of the Niger Delta" in E.A. Alagoa, F.N. Anozie and N. Nzewunwa (eds.). *The Early History of the Niger Delta.* Hamburg: Helmut Buske. pp. 68-119.

APPENDICES

APPENDIX I

OGONI BILL OF RIGHTS

PRESENTED TO THE
GOVERNMENT AND PEOPLE
OF NIGERIA
October, 1990

WITH

AN APPEAL TO THE INTERNATIONAL COMMUNITY

by

The Movement for the Survival of Ogoni People (MOSOP) December, 1991

Published by Saros International Publishers, 24 Aggrey Road, P O B Box 193, Port Harcourt, Nigeria for the Movement for the Survival of Ogoni People (MOSOP) June 1992.

FOREWORD

In August 1990, the Chiefs and people of Ogoni in Nigeria met to sign one of the most important declarations to come out of Africa in recent times: *The Ogoni Bill of Rights*. By the Bill, the Ogoni people, while underlining their loyalty to the Nigerian nation, laid claim as a people to their independence which British colonialism had first violated and then handed over to some other Nigerian ethnic groups in October 1960.

The Bill of Rights presented to the Government and people of Nigeria called for political control of Ogoni affairs by Ogoni people, control and use of Ogoni economic resources for Ogoni development, adequate and direct representation as of right of Ogoni people in Nigerian national institutions and the right to protect the Ogoni environment and ecology from further degradation.

Those rights which should have reverted to the Ogoni after the termination of British rule, have been usurped in the past thirty years by the majority ethnic groups of Nigeria. They have not only been usurped; they have been misused and abused, turning Nigeria into a hell on earth for the Ogoni and similar ethnic minorities. Thirty years of Nigerian independence has done no more than outline the wretched quality of the leadership of the Nigerian majority ethnic groups and their cruelty as they have plunged the nation into ethnic strife, carnage, war, dictatorship, retrogression and the greatest waste of national resources ever witnessed in world history, turning generations of Nigerians, born and unborn into perpetual debtors. *The Ogoni Bill of Rights* rejects once and for all this incompetent indigenous colonialism and calls for a new order in Nigeria, an order in which each ethnic group will have full responsibility for its own affairs and competition between the various peoples of Nigeria will be fair, thus ushering in a new era of peaceful coexistence, co-operation and national progress. This is the path which has been chosen by the European tribes in the European Community, and by the Russians and their neighbours in the new Commonwealth which they are now fashioning. The Yugoslav tribes are being forced into similar ways. The lesson is that high fences make, good neighbours. The Ogoni people are therefore in the mainstream of international thought.

It is well-known that since the issuance of the *Bill of Rights* the Babangida administration has continued in the reactionary ways of all the military rulers of Nigeria from Ironsi through Gowon, Obasanjo and Buhari, seeking to turn Nigeria into a unitary state against the wishes of the Nigerian peoples and trends in world history. The split of the country into 30 states and 600 local governments in 1991 is a waste of resources, a veritable exercise in futility. It is a further attempt to transfer the seized resources of the Ogoni and other minority ethnic groups in the delta to the majority ethnic groups of the country. Without oil, these states and local governments will not exist for one day longer.

The import of the creation of these states is that the Ogoni and other minority groups will continue to be slaves of the majority ethnic groups. It is a gross abuse of human rights, a notably undemocratic act which flies in the face of modern history. The Ogoni people are right to reject it. While they are willing, for the reasons of Africa, to share their resources with other Africans, they insist that it must be on the principles of mutuality, of fairness, of equity and justice.

It has been assumed that because the Ogoni are few in number, they can be abused and denied their rights and that their environment can be destroyed without compunction. This has been the received wisdom of Nigeria according to military dictatorships. 1992 will put paid to this as the Ogoni put their case to the international community.

It is the intention of the Ogoni people to draw the attention of the American government and people to the fact that the oil which they buy from Nigeria is stolen property and that it is against American law to receive stolen goods.

The Ogoni people will be telling the European Community that their demand of the Yugoslav tribes that they respect human rights, minority rights and democracy should also apply to Nigeria and that they should not wait for Nigeria to burst into ethnic strife and carnage before enjoining these civilised values on a Nigeria which depends on European investment, technology and credit.

The Ogoni people will be appealing to the British Government and the leaders of the Commonwealth who have urged on Commonwealth countries the virtues of good government, democracy, human rights and environmental protection which cheat a section of its peoples; that democracy does not exist where laws do not protect minorities and that the environment of the Ogoni and other delta minorities has been ruined beyond repair by multi-national oil companies under the protection of administrations run by Nigerians of the majority ethnic groups.

The Ogoni people will make representation to the World Bank and the International Monetary Fund to the effect that giving loans and credit to the Nigerian Government on the understanding that oil money will be used to repay such loans is to encourage the Nigerian government to continue to dehumanize the Ogoni people and to devastate the environment and ecology of the Ogoni and other delta minorities among whom oil is found.

The Ogoni people will inform the United Nations and the Organization of African Unity that the Nigerian Constitution and the actions of the power elite in Nigeria flagrantly violate the UN Declaration of Human Rights and the African Charter of Human and Peoples Rights; and that Nigeria in 1992 is no different from Apartheid South Africa. The Ogoni people will ask that Nigeria be duly chastized by both organizations for its inhuman actions and uncivilized behaviour. And if Nigeria persists in its perversity, then it should be expelled from both organizations.

These actions of the Ogoni people aim at the restoration of the inalienable rights of the Ogoni people as a distinct ethnic community in Nigeria, and at the establishment of a democratic Nigeria, a progressive, multi-ethnic nation, a realistic society of equals, a just, nation.

What the Ogoni demand for then:selves, namely, autonomy, they also ask for others throughout Nigeria and, indeed, the continent of Africa.

It is their hope the international community will respond to these just demands as they have done to similar demands in other parts of the world.

Ken Saro-Wiwa
Port Harcourt, 24/12/91

STATEMENT BY DR. G.B. LETON, OON, JP

President of the Movement for the Survival of Ogoni People (MOSOP)

The Ogoni case is of genocide being committed in the dying years of the twentieth century by multinational oil companies under the supervision of the Government of the Federal Republic of Nigeria. It is that of a distinct ethnic minority in Nigeria who feel so suffocated by existing political, economic and social conditions in Nigeria that they have no choice, but to cry out to the international community for salvation.

2. The Ogoni are a distinct ethnic group inhabiting the coastal plains terraces to the north-east of the Niger delta. On account of the hitherto very rich plateau soil, the people are mainly subsistence farmers but they also engage in migrant and nomadic fishing. They occupy an area of about 400 square miles and number an estimated 500,000. The population density of about 1,250 persons per square mile is among the highest in any rural area of the world and compares with the Nigerian national average of 300. The obvious problem is the pressure on land.

3. Petroleum was discovered in Ogoni at Bomu (Dere) in 1958; since then an estimated US 100 billion dollars worth of oil has been carted away from Ogoniland. In return for this, the Ogoni have no pipe-borne water, no electricity, very few roads, ill-equipped schools and hospitals and no industry whatsoever.

4. Ogoni has suffered and continues to suffer the degrading effects of oil exploration and exploitation: lands, streams and

creeks are totally and continually polluted; the atmosphere is for ever charged with hydrocarbons, carbon monoxide and carbon dioxide; many villages experience the infernal quaking of the wrath of gas flares which have been burning 24 hours a day for 33 years!; acid rain, oil spillages and blow-outs are common. The results of such unchecked environmental pollution and degradation are that (i) The Ogoni can no longer farm successfully. Once the food basket of the eastern Niger delta, the Ogoni now buy food (when they can afford it); (ii) Fish once a common source of protein, is now rare. Owing to the constant and continual pollution of our streams and creeks, fish can only be caught in deeper and offshore waters for which the Ogoni are not equipped. (iii) All wildlife is dead. (iv) The ecology is changing fast. The mangrove tree, the aerial roots of which normally provide a natural and welcome habitat for many a sea food - crabs, periwinkles, mudskippers, cockles, mussels, shrimps and all - is now being gradually replaced by unknown and otherwise useless palms. (v) The health hazards generated by an atmosphere charged with hydrocarbon vapour, carbon monoxide and carbon dioxide are innumerable.

5. The once beautiful Ogoni countryside is no more a source of fresh air and green vegetation. All one sees and feels around is death. Death is everywhere in Ogoni. Ogoni languages are dying; Ogoni culture is dying; Ogoni people, Ogoni animals, Ogoni fishes are dying because of 33 years of hazardous environmental pollution and resulting food scarcity. In spite of an alarming density of population, American and British oil companies greedily encroach on more and more Ogoni land,

depriving the peasants of their only means of livelihood. Mining rents and royalties for Ogoni oil are seized by the Federal Government of Nigeria which offers the Ogoni people NOTHING in return. Ogoni is being killed so that Nigeria can live.

6. Politically, the Ogoni are being ground to the dust under dictatorial decrees imposed by successive military regimes in Nigeria and laws smuggled by military dictatorships into the Nigerian Constitution which Constitution does not protect ethnic minorities and which today bears no resemblance whatsoever to the covenant entered into by the federating Nigerian ethnic groups at Independence.

7. Ethnicity is a fact of Nigerian life. Nigeria is a federation of ethnic groups. In practice, however, ethnocentrism is the order of the day in the country. The rights and resources of the Ogoni have been usurped by the majority ethnic groups and the Ogoni consigned to slavery and possible extinction. The Ogoni people reject the current political and administrative structuring of Nigeria imposed by the Military Government. They believe with Obafemi Awolowo that "in a true federation, each ethnic group, no matter how small is entitled to the same treatment as any other ethnic group, no matter how large."

8. The Ogoni people therefore demand POLITICAL AUTONOMY as a distinct and separate unit of the Nigerian federation - autonomy will guarantee them certain basic rights essential to their survival as a people. This demand has been spelt out in *the Ogoni Bill of Rights*. The Ogoni people stand by

the Bill and now appeal to the international community, as a last resort, to save them from extinction.

(Sgd.) Dr G.B. Leton
President, Movement for the
Survival of the Ogoni People (MOSOP).

OGONI BILL OF RIGHTS

PRESENTED TO THE GOVERNMENT AND PEOPLE OF NIGERIA

We, the people of Ogoni (Babbe, Gokana, Kekana, Yõkana and Tee) numbering about 500,000 being a separate and distinct ethnic nationality within the Federal Republic of Nigeria, wish to draw the attention of the Governments and people of Nigeria to the undermentioned facts:

1. That the Ogoni people, before the advent of British colonialism, were not conquered or colonized by any other ethnic group in present-day Nigeria.
2. That British colonization forced us into the administrative division of Opobo from 1908 to 1947.
3. That we protested against this forced union until the Ogoni Native Authority was created in 1947 and placed under the then Rivers Province.
4. That in 1951 we were forcibly included in the Eastern Region of Nigeria where we suffered utter neglect.
5. That we protested against this neglect by voting against the party in power in the Region in 1957, and against the forced union by testimony before the Willink Commission of Inquiry into Minority fears in 1958.
6. That this protest led to the inclusion of our nationality in Rivers State in 1967, which State consists of several ethnic nationalities with differing cultures, languages and aspirations.

7. That oil was struck and produced in commercial quantities on our land in 1958 at K. Dere (Bomu oil field).
8. That oil has been mined on our land since 1958 to this day from the following oil fields: (i) Bomu (ii) Bodo West (iii) Tee (Tai) (iv) Korokoro (v) Yorla (vi) Lubara Creek and (vii) Afam by Shell Petroleum Development Company (Nigeria) Limited.
9. That in over 30 years of oil mining, the Ogoni nationality have provided the Nigerian nation with a total revenue estimated at over 40 billion Naira (N40 billion) or 30 billion dollars.
10. That in return for the above contribution, the Ogoni people have received NOTHING.
11. That today, the Ogoni people have:
    (i) No representation whatsoever in ALL institutions of the Federal Government of Nigeria.
    (ii) No pipe-borne water.
    (iii) No electricity.
    (iv) No job opportunities for the citizens in Federal, State, public sector or private sector companies.
    (v) No social or economic project of the Federal Government.
12. That the Ogoni languages of Gokana and Kana are underdeveloped and are about to disappear, whereas other Nigerian languages are being forced on us.

13. That the ethnic policies of successive Federal and State Governments are gradually pushing the Ogoni people to slavery and possible extinction.
14. That the Shell Petroleum Development Company of Nigeria Limited does not employ Ogoni people at a meaningful or any level at all, in defiance of the Federal government's regulations.
15. That the search for oil has caused severe land and food shortages in Ogoni, one of the most densely populated areas of Africa (average: 1,500 per square mile; national average: 300 per square mile).
16. The neglected environmental pollution laws and sub-standard inspection techniques of the Federal authorities have led to the complete degradation of the Ogoni environment, turning our homeland into an ecological disaster.
17. That the Ogoni people lack education, health and other social facilities.
18. That it is intolerable that one of the richest areas of Nigeria should wallow in abject poverty and destitution.
19. The successive Federal administrations have trampled on every minority right enshrined in the Nigerian Constitution to the detriment of the Ogoni and have by administrative structuring and other noxious acts transferred Ogoni wealth exclusively to other parts of the Republic.
20. That the Ogoni people wish to manage their own affairs.

Now, therefore, while reaffirming our wish to remain a part of the Federal Republic of Nigeria, we make demand upon the Republic as follows:

That the Ogoni people be granted POLITICAL AUTONOMY to participate in the affairs of the Republic as a distinct and separate unit by whatever name called, provided that the Autonomy guarantees the following:

(a) Political control of Ogoni affairs by Ogoni people.
(b) The right to the control and use of a fair proportion of OGONI economic resources for Ogoni development.
(c) Adequate and direct representation as of right in all Nigerian national institutions.
(d) The use and development of Ogoni languages in Ogoni territory.
(e) The full development of Ogoni culture.
(f) The right to religious freedom.
(g) The right to protect the OGONI environment and ecology from further degradation.

We make the above demand in the knowledge that it does not deny any other ethnic group in the Nigerian Federation of their rights and that it can only conduce to peace, justice and fair play and hence stability and progress in the Nigerian nation.

We make the above demand in the belief that, as Obafemi Awolowo has written: *In a true Federation, each ethnic group no matter how small, is entitled to the same treatment as any other ethnic group, no matter how large.*

We demand these rights as equal members of the Nigerian Federation who contribute and have contributed to the growth of the Federation and have a right to expect full returns from that Federation.

Adopted by general acclaim of the Ogoni people on the 26th day of August, 1990 at Bori, Rivers State and signed by: (see under).

ADDENDUM TO THE OGONI BILL OF RIGHTS

We, the people of Ogoni, being a separate and distinct ethnic nationality within the Federal republic of Nigeria, hereby state as follows:

A. That on October 2, 1990 we addressed an "Ogoni Bill of Rights" to the President of the Federal republic of Nigeria, General Ibrahim Babaginda and members of the Armed Forces Ruling Council;

B. That after a one-year wait, the President has been unable to grant us the audience which we sought to have with him in order to discuss the legitimate demands contained in the Ogoni Bill of Rights;

C. That our demands as outlined in the Ogoni Bill of Rights are legitimate, just and inalienable right and in accord with civilized values world-wide;

D. That the Government of the Federal republic of Nigeria has continued, since October 2, 1990, to decree measures and implement policies which further marginalize the Ogoni people, denying us political autonomy, our rights to our resources, to the development of our languages and culture, to adequate representation as of right in all Nigerian national institutions and to the protection of our environment and ecology from further degradation;

E. That we cannot sit idly by while we are, as a people, dehumanized and slowly exterminated and driven to extinction even as our rich resources are siphoned off to the exclusive comfort and improvement of other Nigerian communities, and the shareholders of multinational oil companies.

Now therefore, while re-affirming our wish to remain a part of the Federal Republic of Nigeria, we hereby authorize the Movement for the Survival of Ogoni People (MOSOP) to make representation, for as long as these injustices continue, to the United Nations Commission on Human Rights, the Commonwealth Secretariat, the African Commission on Human and Peoples' Rights, the European Community and all international bodies which have a role to play in the preservation of our nationality, as follows:

1. That the Government of the Federal Republic of Nigeria has, in utter disregard and contempt for human rights, since independence in 1960 till date, denied us our political rights to self-determination, economic rights to our resources, cultural rights to the development of our languages and culture, and social rights to education, health and adequate housing and to representation as of right in national institutions;

2. That, in particular, the Federal Republic of Nigeria has refused to pay us royalties and mining rents amounting to an estimated 20 billion US dollars for petroleum mined from our soil for over thirty-three years;

3. That the Constitution of the Federal Republic of Nigeria does not protect any of our rights whatsoever as an ethnic minority of 500,000 in a nation of about 100 million people and that the voting power and military might of the majority ethnic groups have been used remorselessly against us at every point in time;

4. That multi-national oil companies, namely Shell (Dutch/British) and Chevron (American) have severally and jointly devastated our environment and ecology, having flared gas in our villages for 33 years and caused oil spillages, blow-outs etc., and have dehumanized our people, denying them employment and those benefits which industrial organizations in Europe and America routinely contribute to their areas of operation;

5. That the Nigerian elite (bureaucratic, military, industrial and academic) have turned a blind eye and a deaf ear to these acts of dehumanization by the ethnic majority and have colluded with all the agents of destruction aimed at us;

6. That we cannot seek restitution in the courts of law in Nigeria as the act of expropriation of our rights and resources has been institutionalized in the 1979 and 1989 Constitutions of the Federal Republic of Nigeria, which Constitutions were acts of a Constituent Assembly imposed by a military regime and do not, in any way, protect minority rights or bear resemblance to the tacit agreement made at Nigerian independence;

7. That the Ogoni people abjure violence in their just struggle for their rights within the Federal Republic of Nigeria but will, through every lawful means, and for as long as is necessary, fight for social justice and equity for themselves and their progeny, and in particular demand political autonomy as a distinct and separate unit within the Nigerian nation with full right to (i) control Ogoni political affairs, (ii) use at least fifty per cent of Ogoni economic resources for Ogoni development; (iii) protect the Ogoni environment and ecology from further degradation; (iv) ensure the full restitution of the harm done to the health of our people by the flaring of gas, oil spillages, oil blow-outs, etc. by the following oil companies: Shell, Chevron and their Nigerian accomplices.

8. That without the intervention of the international community, the Government of the Federal Republic of Nigeria and the ethnic majority will continue these noxious policies until the Ogoni people are obliterated from the face of the earth.

Adopted by general acclaim of the Ogoni people on the 26th day of August 1991 at Bori, Rivers State of Nigeria.

Signed on behalf of the Ogoni people by:
BABBE: HRH Mark Tsaro-Igbara, Gbenemene Babbe; HRH F.M.K. Noryaa, Menebua, Ka-Babbe; Chief M.A.M. Tornwe III, JP; Prince J.S. Sangha; Dr Israel Kue; Chief A.M.N. Gua.

GOKANA: HRH James P. Bagia, Gberesako XI, Gbenemene Gokana; Chief E.N. Kobani, JP, Tonsimene Gokana; Dr. B.N. Birabi; Chief Kemte Giadom, JP; Chief S.N. Orage.

KEKANA: HRH M.H.S. Eguru, Gbenemene Kekana; HRH C.B.S. Nwikina, Emah III, Menebua Bom; Mr M.C. Daanwii; Chief T.N. Nwieke; Mr Ken Saro-Wiwa; Mr Simeon Idemyor.

YÕKANA: HRH W.Z.P. Nzidee, Genemene Bãa I of Yõkana; Dr G.B. Leton, OON, JP; Mr Lekue Lah-Loolo; Mr L.E. Mwara; Chief E.A. Apenu; Pastor M.P. Maeba.

TEE: HRH B.A. Mballey, Gbenemene Tee; HRH G.N. Gininwa, Menebua Tua Tua; Chief J.S. Agbara; Chief D.J.K. Kumbe; Chief Fred Gwezia; HRH A. Demor-Kanni, Menebua Nonwa.

THE INTERNATIONAL COMMUNITY SHOULD:

1. Prevail on the American Government to stop buying Nigerian oil. It is stolen property.
2. Prevail on Shell and Chevron to stop flaring gas in Ogoni.
3. Prevail on the Federal Government of Nigeria to honour the rights of the Ogoni people to self-determination and AUTONOMY.
4. Prevail on the Federal Government of Nigerian to pay all royalties and mining rents collected on oil mined from Ogoni since 1958.
5. Prevail on the World Bank and the International Monetary Fund to stop giving loans to the Federal

Government of Nigeria; all loans which depend for their repayment on the exploitation of Ogoni oil resource.

6. Send urgent medical and other aid to the Ogoni people.

7. Prevail on the United Nations, the organization of African Unity and the Commonwealth of Nations to either get the Federal Government of Nigeria to obey the rules and mores of these organizations, face sanctions or be expelled from them.

8. Prevail on European and American Governments to stop giving aid and credit to the Federal Government of Nigeria as aid and credit only go to encourage the further dehumanization of the Ogoni people.

9. Prevail on European and American Governments to grant political refugee status to all Ogoni people seeking protection from the political persecution and genocide at the hands of the Federal Government of Nigeria.

10. Prevail on Shell and Chevron to pay compensation to the Ogoni people for ruining the Ogoni environment and the health of Ogoni men, women and children.

APPENDIX II

CONSTITUTION OF THE MOVEMENT FOR THE SURVIVAL OF OGONI PEOPLE

1. **Name:**
   The name of the organization shall be Movement for the Survival of Ogoni People (MOSOP).
2. **Aims and Objectives:**
   (a) To seek Autonomy for Ogoni people within the Nigerian Federation.
   (b) To promote the well-being of all Ogoni people.
   (c) To ensure that Ogoni people survive as a distinct ethnic group in Nigeria with all their rights respected.
   (d) To co-operate with all other Nigerian ethnic groups.
   (e) To seek the evolution of a Nigerian nation of equals.

Note: (i) MOSOP shall not involve itself in partisan politics.
   Members may belong to any political party of their wish but must promote Ogoni interest wherever they may be.
   (ii) The Movement shall use non-violent means to achieve its aims.

3. **Membership:**
   There shall be two categories of membership.
   (i) **Individual Membership:** Open to all Ogoni people including women of other ethnic groups married to Ogoni people.
   (ii) Honorary Membership: Persons who may not be Ogoni, but may have made notable contribution to the survival of of Ogoni people may be made honorary members.

4. **Headquarters:**
   Shall be at Bori. Members of the Movement in a State, city or town outside of Ogoni shall be free to establish an office or branch of the Movement in their locality.

5. **Finances:**
   Membership dues shall be as follows:
   Registration fee of ₦10.00.
   Annual subscription of ₦20.00 per year.
   In addition there will be a levy.

Structure and Functions:
(i) Quarterly general meeting of all members of the Movement. An Annual Congress shall be the highest authority of the Movement and subject to that authority an Executive Committee shall be elected to manage the affairs of the Movement between Congresses.
(ii) The Congress shall set up, as it may deem necessary, special committees in pursuit of its objectives, and any

such committee shall be free to co-opt specialists to assist in its work.

(iii) The Executive: Shall consist of the following officers to be elected at the Congress: President, 5 Vice-Presidents (one from each Ogoni Kingdom), General Secretary, 2 Assistant Secretaries, Treasurer, Legal Adviser, 2 Publicity Secretaries, 5 other members, one Financial Secretary, Chairmen of Local Governments in the area, 2 Auditors.

(iv) Branches may be established anywhere there are ten or more members. Such a branch shall elect their own officers and hold meetings as may be necessary or convenient.

(v) Decisions at meetings of the organization including Congress, shall be by simple majority voting provided that where a meeting is not possible, the Executive Committee may canvass members by post or other means to obtain their views.

Quorum: Executive Committee shall be ⅓; Congress ¼.

Financial Regulations:

(a) The Movement shall open a bank account into which all monies (except a maximum of one thousand naira to be held by the Treasurer or General Secretary for imprest) shall be paid.

(b) The Treasurer, General Secretary and the President of the Movement shall be signatories to the said bank account.

(c) The Treasurer shall keep proper books of account in respect of all receipts and payments made in respect of the Movement's account.
(d) Thirty (30) days before the fourth quarterly general meeting, the Treasurer shall submit his books of account to the Auditors who shall audit same.
(e) The report of the auditors shall be presented to the fourth quarterly congress of the Movement.

Amendment of Constitution:

The Constitution of the Movement may be amended at any Congress by a two-thirds majority vote of the registered members.

Congress:

Shall be attended by individual members and village members. Individual members shall have a single vote. Three (3) members shall represent each village (The Chief, a man and a woman). Each village shall have a single vote.

Dissolution:

(a) The Movement may dissolve itself by a three-quarters majority vote of the entire membership voting at an annual congress.
(b) Thereafter all monies and property belonging to the Movement shall be donated to charity.

APPENDIX III

STATEMENT BY PHILIP ASIODU
(One time Permanent Secretary, Federal Ministry of Mines and Power)

Like [sic] in many other areas of the world, the regions where oil is found in this country (NIGERIA) are very inhospitable. They are mainly in swamps and creeks. They require massive injection of money if their conditions and standards of living are to compare with what attains elsewhere in the country where the possibilities of agriculture and diversified industry are much greater. There is a nudging acceptance of the special needs of oil areas in the latest proposals being discussed by the government but I believe there is a long way to go to meet the claims of the oil-producing areas which see themselves losing non-replaceable resources while replaceable and permanent resources of agriculture and industry are being developed elsewhere largely with oil revenue. Given, however, the small size and population of the oil-producing areas, it is not cynical to observe that even if the resentments of oil producing states continue, they cannot threaten the stability of the country nor affect its continued economic development.

> - Mr Philip Asiodu in a Public Lecture to Nigerian civil servants in 1980. Mr Philip Asiodu was once a powerful Permanent Secretary in the Federal Ministry of Mines and Power in Lagos, Nigeria. He is currently a Director of Chevron Oil Company.

www.ingramcontent.com/pod-product-compliance
Lightning Source LLC
Chambersburg PA
CBHW071405290426
44108CB00014B/1687